...THE...
LEBANON
COOK BOOK

Compiled from
Recipes
Collected by the
Ladies of the
Centenary M. E. Church

HERITAGE BOOKS
2007

HERITAGE BOOKS
AN IMPRINT OF HERITAGE BOOKS, INC.

Books, CDs, and more—Worldwide

For our listing of thousands of titles see our website
at
www.HeritageBooks.com

A Facsimile Reprint
Published 2007 by
HERITAGE BOOKS, INC.
Publishing Division
65 East Main Street
Westminster, Maryland 21157-5026

Originally published

Lebanon, Pa.
Report Publishing Company, Ltd., Printers
1896

— Publisher's Notice —
In reprints such as this, it is often not possible to remove blemishes from the original. We feel the contents of this book warrant its reissue despite these blemishes and hope you will agree and read it with pleasure.

International Standard Book Number: 978-0-7884-4297-X

The Cake
will be Spoiled

IF THE INGREDIENTS are not pure. Pure Cream of Tartar, Baking Soda, Spices and Flavoring are an essential to good baking.

We have them *absolutely pure*. You can tell the difference only after you have used them. The safe way is to buy them where you know you will get *the best, before you use them.*

Everything at our store is PURE. Our Cooking Spices, our Flavoring Extracts, our Soda and Cream of Tartar, our Drugs and Medicines, our Perfumery and Soaps.

Whenever you want anything in these lines, don't forget that we have been in the business almost 50 years, and know how and where to get the best goods. They cost you no more than poor quality.

Dr. Geo. Ross & Co.
DRUGGISTS,

Opposite Court House. Lebanon, Pa

OUR OWN { Cold Boiled Ham.
Potted Ham.
Potted Tongue.
Pickled Spiced Celery.

Full Assortment of Canned Goods.

BOTTLED { Pickles.
Olives.
Chow Chow.

Full Assortment of Cakes and Crackers at our place for pic-nics.
Eagle Butter Cracker the best to fry.
Remember our Grocery and call on us.

BENSING & BRO., Grocers, 38 S. 9th St.

 # J. K. KNERR,
Dealer in Best Grades of
.....Family Coal.

COAL

 Yard : **214** North 8th Street.

Residence, 408 Chestnut St., Lebanon, Pa.

Palms and Ornamental Foliage Plants
...For Sale and to Let...

Mish's

Lebanon Valley

Green=

houses

Chestnut and Fourth Sts.
and South Front St.

....Carnations a Specialty....

Frantz's Furniture Bazaar.

The Largest Assortment of Furniture in the City at the LOWEST PRICES.

SPECIAL INDUCEMENTS GIVEN TO YOUNG HOUSEKEEPERS.

All Goods Delivered Free.

Ware Rooms---Nos. 732 and 734 Cumberland Street, LEBANON, PA.

John A. Sherk & Co.,
No. 430 North 11th Street.

Headquarters for....

GASOLINE
And Best Grades of **OIL.**

You will find our prices the lowest and quality the best.

GOODS DELIVERED TO ALL PARTS OF THE CITY.

Drop us a postal and we will call.

PLEASE GIVE US ....A TRIAL. SATISFACTION GUARANTEED.

WHY NOT BUY

THE FINEST AND BEST  ...Organ

Made, especially when you can get it at the same price as other Organs are sold for. Intending purchasers should send to us for Catalogue, etc.

We are also General Agents for the

Krakauer Piano.

150 Of these Pianos in use in the City of Lebanon alone. It is the Finest and Best Piano made. Catalogues, etc., free. . . . .

Miller Organ Co.
LEBANON, PA.

EDWARD R. COLEMAN, *President.*
B. DAWSON COLEMAN, *Vice-President.*
JOHN H. HOFFER, *Cashier.*

The First National Bank

No. 240...

...Directors...

HORACE BROCK.   B. DAWSON COLEMAN.
ARTHUR BROCK.   EDWARD R. COLEMAN.
           J. P. S. GOBIN.

The Largest and Cheapest in America.

Mackintoshes and Clothing

........FOR........

Gentlemen and Ladies.

Made-to-Measure AND **Ready-to-Wear.**

BEST QUALITY.
LATEST STYLES.
LOWEST PRICES.

O. DETWEILER,
Sales Agent for Wanamaker & Brown,

630 Cumberland Street, - - - LEBANON, PA.

It is a Pleasure

TO ANY HOUSEWIFE TO PLACE UPON HER TABLE ....

Fine Silverware.

We have at any and all times an elegant variety of Sterling Silver, and the finest quality of silverplated

Knives, Forks, Spoons, Butter Dishes, Tea Sets, Etc.

Our well-known reputation for square dealing always a guarantee on all our goods. It's a good thing to deal with a house you know.

J. K. LAUDERMILCH, The Reliable Jeweler,
Established Over 30 Years.   844 Cumberland Street, LEBANON, PA.

Looking Backward

May be a pleasing pastime, but we take pleasure in "Looking Forward" to the time when the growing population of this City will all have become convinced that the best place to buy all kinds of . . . .

...Novelties...

Dinner and Tea Sets, Toilet Sets, Glass and Queensware, Tinware, Lamps, Window Shades, Notions, Dolls, Toys, etc., is at the . . . .

Boston Novelty Store

736 Cumberland Street,

JAS. H. ROBERTS, PROPRIETOR.

Lebanon, Pa.

John Reinoehl.....

Dry Goods, Notions, Oil-Cloths, Groceries —Queensware, Etc.

14 SOUTH NINTH STREET
...Eagle Building...   LEBANON, PA.

Erb & Craumer
Hats and
...Men's Fine Furnishings

Umbrellas
Trunks
Satchels
Ties
Handkerchiefs
Hose
Shirts
Night Shirts
Mackintoshes
Hats
Underwear
Gloves, &c.

Cor. 8th and Cumberland Sts.

Opposite Court House   Nutting Building

Sole Agents for...
    Youman Hats
    Manhattan and Paris
    Dress Shirts,
    Dent's Gloves, Etc.

Established 1872.   Oldest Stand in the City.

M. & C. Duth

Carry
All Grades
of
Seasonable

Millinery.

Lowest
Prices.

GIVE US A CALL.

712
Cumberland Street,

LEBANON,
PENN'A.

※ TRIED, TESTED, PROVED. ※

...THE...

LEBANON COOK BOOK

COMPILED FROM RECIPES COLLECTED BY THE
LADIES OF CENTENARY M. E. CHURCH.

Published for the Benefit of Centenary M. E. Church.

LEBANON, PA.
REPORT PUBLISHING COMPANY, LTD., PRINTERS.
1896.

TABLE OF MEASURES.

1 Quart of Wheat Flour, - - - - 1 pound.
1 Quart of Indian Meal, - - - - 1 ℔. 4 oz.
1 Pint of Soft Butter, well packed, - - - 1 pound.
1 Pint of Loaf Sugar, - - - - - 1 pound.
10 Eggs, - - - - - - - 1 pound.
40 Drops, - - - - - - 1 Teaspoonful.
4 Tablespoonfuls, - - - - - 1 Wine Glass.
4 Gills, - - - - - - - - 1 Pint.
2 Teaspoonfuls, - - - - - 1 Tablespoonful.
16 Large Tablespoonfuls, - - - - $\frac{1}{2}$ Pint.
A Common-Sized Tumbler holds - - - $\frac{1}{2}$ Pint.
A Common-Sized Wine Glass, - - - - $\frac{1}{2}$ Gill.
4 Teacupfuls, - - - - - - - 1 Quart.
Butter, size of an Egg, - - - - - 2 Ounces.

Apothegm.

We may live without poetry, music and art;
We may live without conscience, and live without heart;
We may live without friends, we may live without books;
But civilized man cannot live without cooks.

  He may live without books—
   What is knowledge but giving?
  He may live without hope—
   What is hope but deceiving?
  He may live without love—
   What is passion but pining?
  But where is the man
   That can live without dining?

"Good cooking means economy and enjoyment.
Bad cooking means waste of money, time and temper."

We Can Save You Money.

WE ARE LEADERS IN LOW PRICES AND BEST QUALITIES.

We Have The Largest Assortment of  Caps and Gents' Furnishing Goods in the City at the Very Lowest Prices.

We buy all goods direct from the manufacturer for spot cash.

BACHRACH BROS., No. 747 Cumberland Street.

Bachrach Bros. Hats are the BEST.

ATKINS & BRO.,

DEALERS IN

Choice Family Groceries

FINE TEAS AND COFFEES.

Pure Spices and Baking Powders A Specialty.

No. 20 South Ninth St., - - - - LEBANON, PA.

SOUPS.

"Now good digestion wait on appetite, and health on both."
—Shakespeare.

Clam Soup.
Mrs. J. K. Fisher.

1 quart of water, 1 dozen clams chopped fine, 2 potatoes diced, 1 cup of milk, not put in until done; ½ dozen whole allspice, butter, size of a walnut, browned; pepper and salt to taste, 1 hard-boiled egg, cut fine; add a little celery seed.

Clam Soup.
Elizabeth Hammond Hoffer.

25 medium-sized clams, cut small; 3 pints of water, 1 onion, chopped fine. Boil 15 minutes. Add thickening of 1 tablespoonful of butter and 2 of flour. Boil a few minutes. Take from the fire and add 1 pint of milk, which has been beaten up with the yolks of four eggs. Stir while adding the milk and eggs, and serve without any more boiling.

Clam Chowder.
Mrs. J. D. Keefer, Columbia, Pa.,

12 nice clams, chopped fine, with broth from same; add 1 quart of water. Boil 15 minutes, then add about 4 potatoes, chopped or cut fine; 1 pint of peas, 1 pint of corn, 2 hard-boiled eggs, chopped fine; 1 pint of milk. Then make butter balls or add crackers to thicken. Boil a few minutes; then ready to serve in soup plates. Season well.

Clam Broth.

Boil 25 clams in their liquor, strain, add pepper and chopped parsley.

Onion Soup.
Mrs. Helen Campbell.

Take 3 large onions, slice them very thin, and then fry to a bright brown in a large spoonful of either butter or stock fat, the latter answering equally well. When brown, add ½ teacupful of flour, and stir constantly until red. Then pour slowly 1 pint of boiling water, stirring steadily till it is all in. Boil and mash 4 large potatoes, and stir into 1 quart of boiling milk, taking care that there are no lumps. Add this to the fried onions, with 1 teaspoonful of salt ½ teaspoonful of white pepper. Let all boil for 5 minutes, and then serve with toasted or fried bread. Simple as this seems, it is one of the best of the vegetable soups, though it is made richer by the use of stock instead of water.

Pea Soup.

1 quart of dried peas, washed and soaked over night; split peas are best. In the morning put them on the fire, with 6 quarts of cold water, 1 even tablespoonful of salt, 1 saltspoonful of cayenne, and 1 teaspoonful of celery seed. Fry till a bright brown three onions, cut small, and add to the peas. Cover closely and boil 4 or 5 hours. Strain through a colander, and, if not perfectly smooth, return to fire and add a thickening, made of 1 heaping teaspoonful of flour and an even 1 of butter, stirred together with a little hot water and boiled 5 minutes. Beans can be used in precisely the same way; and both bean and pea soups are nicer served with croutons.

Cream Potato Soup.
Mrs. W. T. Richardson.

1 quart of fresh milk, 6 large potatoes, 1 stalk of celery, 1 small onion (if liked). Put milk to boil with celery. Pare potatoes and boil 30 minutes. Then mash them fine and light and add the boiling milk. Butter, salt and pepper to taste. Rub through a strainer and serve immediately. When in tureen add 1 cup of whipped cream as an improvement.

Oyster Soup.

Strain the liquor from a quart of oysters; add 1 cup of water, and let the two become scalding hot, using a double boiler. Then add a quart of milk and when this boils, add 2 tablespoonfuls of butter, rubbed into 1 tablespoonful of flour. Add lastly the oysters, and let them cook 3 minutes. Season to taste with a little salt and white pepper, and serve very hot. This receipt makes a sufficient amount for 6 or 8 persons.

Tomato Soup.
Mrs. W. S. Donnan.

Stew 1 quart of peeled tomatoes and ½ teaspoonful of soda until thoroughly cooked. Pour this into a ½ gallon of boiling milk (fresh), stirring well. Season with red pepper, salt, and a teaspoonful of butter. Just before serving, thicken with rolled crackers. A little sugar may be added.

Tomato Soup.
Maze Johnson.

Boil a can of tomatoes until thoroughly cooked, and press through a sieve. To this add ½ teaspoonful of soda. Put into a saucepan a piece of butter, size of an egg, with a tablespoonful of flour, mixed smooth. Then add a pint of milk. When this has boiled and thickened, add the tomato pulp, very hot. Do not boil. The soda, mixed with the tomato, prevents the milk from curdling.

Cream Tomato Soup.

To 1 can of tomatoes add 1½ quarts of milk, butter the size of an egg; add salt and pepper to suit the taste. Heat the tomatoes before adding milk.

Noodles for Soup.
M. A. McFarland.

Rub into 2 eggs as much sifted flour as they absorb. Then roll out as thin as a wafer. Dust over a little flour, and then roll over and over into a roll. Cut off thin slices from the edge of the roll, and shake out into long strips. Put them into the soup lightly, and boil for 10 minutes. Mix about a saltspoonful of salt while mixing the flour.

Noodle Soup.
Emma Kaler Johnson.

Beat 1 egg light, add flour enough to make a stiff dough, a pinch of salt. Roll out very thin; dredge with flour to keep from sticking. Dry, and then roll and cut like straw.

Croutons.

Take slices of bread and remove all the crust. Cut into tiny squares, and brown in the oven. If bread is buttered they will brown more quickly. Can be used in place of crackers in soups.

Calf Head Soup.
Mrs. D. S. Hammond

Boil a calf head in 3 quarts of water until well done. Strain the liquid through a cloth. Pick the meat from the bones. Cut up the tongue and brains. Put back into the water, with a teaspoonful of ground cloves, salt and cayenne pepper, sweet marjoram and summer savoy to taste. Thicken with butter and flour rubbed perfectly smooth. Just before serving, add 4 hard-boiled eggs, chopped fine; force meat balls. Force meat balls are made of veal cutlet, chopped fine, seasoned with salt, pepper, ground cloves and allspice to taste. Roll in balls about the size of a marble, and fry in butter.

Calf Head Soup.
Mrs. Mary C. Gingrich.

Put the calf head on the fire and boil till tender. Pick off the meat; cut fine. Add 4 potatoes, and put in the broth. A lump of butter, the size of an egg; a little water and flour, to make butter balls. Add the brain, sweet marjoram, salt, pepper, whole allspice, $\frac{1}{4}$ pound butter, 2 hard-boiled eggs, chopped fine. Boil until the potatoes are cooked. Add butter balls last. Remove the skin, separate the brain, and wash in cold water before adding to the soup.

Vegetable Soup.
Mrs. H. C. Vosbury.

After boiling a soup-bone or piece of beef until done, add to the broth boiling water to make the amount of soup wanted, and, when boiling again, add a large handful of cabbage, cut fine as for slaw; $\frac{1}{2}$ pint of tomatoes, canned or fresh; peel and slice and add 3 large or 4 small onions, and 2 or 3 potatoes; (Some use $\frac{1}{2}$ teacup of dried or $\frac{1}{2}$ pint of green corn. If dried corn is used, it should be soaked.) Let boil from $\frac{1}{2}$ to $\frac{3}{4}$ of an hour. If you like thickening, stir an egg or yolk with a large spoonful of milk and a teaspoonful of flour in 5 or 10 minutes before taking off. This makes it very rich. Serve with crackers.

Vegetable Soup, Without Meat.

1 carrot, 1 turnip, 1 parsnip, 1 potato, 1 onion, 1 tablespoonful of butter, 2 tablespoonfuls of rice, 2 quarts of cold water, 1 teaspoonful of salt, 1 bay leaf, 1 sprig of parsley. Cut the vegetables into dice. Brown butter and onion in a saucepan, and then put in all the vegetables except the potato; this should not be added until 15 minutes before serving. Let the soup cook slowly for 1 hour. This may be put through a sieve or served in the dice shape.

Chicken Cream Soup.
M. A. McFarland.

Boil an old fowl, with an onion, in 4 quarts of cold water. Take it out and let it get cold. Cut off the whole of the breast and chop it very fine. Mix with the pounded yolks of 2 hard-boiled eggs and rub through a colander; cool and skim; then strain the soup into a soup pot. Season; add the chicken and egg mixture. Simmer 10 minutes, and pour into tureen; then add small cup of boiling milk.

Chicken Jelly, very Nutricious.
Mrs. W. S. Donnan.

1 young chicken, simmered in 1 quart of water until the water is reduced to less than 1 pint. Season with salt. Press the chicken from the liquor, and skim thoroughly. It may be eaten cold or hot.

Chicken Soup
Mrs. Frank Maguire.

1 chicken, 2 slices of middling bacon, 5 pints of water, to be boiled slowly down to 1 quart. Then put in 1 teacup of milk or cream.

Cream or Celery Soup.
Mrs. Frank Maguire.

3 stalks of celery, 1 quart of milk, 1 tablespoonful of butter, 2 tablespoonfuls of flour, 1 pint of water, salt and pepper to taste, a small piece of onion. Wash and cut the celery into small pieces. Boil in the water 30 minutes. Then press it through a colander. Boil the milk in a farina kettle. Add it to the strained celery and water. Rub the butter and flour together, and stir into the boiling soup. Stir constantly until it thickens.

Add salt and pepper, and serve at once. Asparagus may be substituted for celery; in this case the heads of the asparagus may be left in the soup.

Chicken Terrapin.
Mrs. Roby.

Boil the chicken. When done, boil the broth down to about a cupful. Cool it; then skim it. When cold, cut the chicken into pieces about ½ inch square, having first skinned the chicken. Put in a frying-pan the broth, 1 cup of milk or cream, ¼ pound of butter, and 2 tablespoonfuls of butter, rubbed smooth. When boiling, add the chicken. Let it cook a moment. Take off the fire and add 2 hard-boiled eggs, chopped.

OYSTERS AND FISH.

"Master, marvel how the fishes live in the sea!"
"Why, as man do a land; the great ones eat up the litle ones."
—Pericles.

Baked Salmon.
Mrs. Henry Houck.

1 can of salmon, strained; 1 pint sweet milk, 3 tablespoonfuls of flour, small lump of butter. Mix well; put on the stove; boil until thick. When cold, beat 2 raw eggs in it. Put the salmon in a pudding dish; pour the dressing over it; put bread-crumbs on top. Bake ½ hour.

Creamed Salmon.
Mrs. J. M. Funck.

Pick a can of salmon; one cup of bread crumbs. Butter a pudding dish, and line with the crumbs. Take a cup of milk, ½ cup of sweet cream, 1 teaspoonful of corn starch, ½ teaspoon soda. Let the milk come to a boil, and thicken with the corn starch. Put in the salmon, and pour in the pudding dish, and cover with the rest of bread crumbs, a little salt and pepper, and bits of butter, and bake until brown.

Scalloped Oysters.

1 pint of oysters, 1 cup of cracker crumbs, 1-3 cup of melted butter, salt and pepper. Prepare the oysters, season with salt

OYSTERS AND FISH.

and pepper. Stir crumbs into the butter. Grease shallow dish, put in ¼ of crumbs, then ½ of oysters, then ¼ crumbs. Remaining oysters and crumbs put on top. Bake 20 minutes, or until crumbs are brown. Bread crumbs may be used.

Oyster Fritters.
H. M. M.

Drain the liquor from the oysters, and to a cupful of this add the same quantity of milk, 3 eggs, a little salt and flour enough for a thin batter. Chop oysters and stir into the batter. Have ready in the frying pan a few tablespoonfuls of lard and butter; heat very hot, and drop the fritters by tablespoonfuls. Take rapidly from pan, as soon as they are done to a pleasing yellow brown. Send to table hot.

Oyster Sauce.
Esther Helms.

2 ounces of butter, 1 stalk celery, 50 oysters, 1 quart milk, 1 spoonful flour.

Chicken Pie With Oysters.

Boil the chicken (a year-old is the best) until tender. Line a dish with a nice crust. Put in chicken; season with salt, pepper and butter; add the liquor, which should be about a pint, in which chicken was boiled; cover loosely with a crust having a slit cut each way in the middle. Drain off liquor from a quart of oysters; boil; skim, season with butter, pepper, salt, and thickening of flour and water, add oysters, boil up once, and (about 20 minutes before the pie is done) lift the crust and put them in.

Devilled Clams.
Mary Hoffer Bowman.

Drain 25 clams from their liquor. This is best done by pouring a cup of cold water over them. Chop fine; scald 1 cup of cream; rub together 1 tablespoonful of butter and 2 of flour until smooth; add to cream and stir until it thickens. Then add 2 tablespoonfuls of bread crumbs, the yolks of 2 raw eggs, 1 tablespoonful of chopped parsley. Take from the fire, mix well together; stir in the clams; pepper and salt to taste. Do not add salt until the clams are mixed, as they may be sufficiently salted. Fill clam shells, brush over with beaten yolk of egg, sprinkle with bread crumbs, and brown in hot oven.

Oyster Pie for Ten.

1 small chicken, 50 oysters, 1 dozen oyster crackers, butter the size of an egg; line a deep baking dish with a rich paste; remove all bones from chicken after having boiled tender; cut in small pieces the size of an oyster; boil hard 3 eggs; cut them in slices. Place one layer of chicken, then oysters, add a few crackers, then egg, and repeat till full. Pepper and salt to taste. Add liquor of oysters and little milk. Bake in a quick oven.

Crumbed Patties.
R. A. C.

Fill small patty pans with oysters, seasoned with pepper, salt and several whole allspice. Spread the top with bread crumbs, which have been fried in butter, and bake in a hot oven 5 minutes. Put sprigs of parsley on each patty.

Oyster Pie.
Mrs. Brunner.

Stew 1 spring chicken, and take the meat from the bones. Add 50 oysters and bake in a deep dish. Pepper and salt to suit taste.

Scalloped Oysters.
Mrs. J. H. Roberts.

Take a layer of cracker crumbs, then a layer of oysters. Continue the same until the dish is filled, with seasoning of salt, pepper and butter with each layer, having cracker crumbs for top layer; adding enough milk to moisten the whole. Put in oven and bake.

Little Pigs in Blankets.
Mrs. D. M. Karmany.

Season large oysters with pepper; roll in rolled crackers; cut bacon in thin slices; wrap an oyster in each slice; fasten with a wooden toothpick; fry just long enough to cook the bacon (about 2 minutes). Serve on small slices of toast, if desired.

Escalloped Oysters.
Mrs. S. H. Reisner.

In a buttered dish place a layer of bread crumbs, then a

layer of oysters, and sprinkle with salt, pepper and bits of butter. Alternate the layers till the dish is nearly full, using crumbs for the top layer. Pour cream or milk, or the two mixed, over the top, and then add more crumbs. Bake, covered, for ½ hour; then uncover and brown. Potatoes are nice prepared in this way, without the crumbs.

Fried Oysters.
Mrs. J. H. Roberts.

Have large, fresh oysters; throw them in a colander to drain. Take one by one and dip in cracker dust. Have ready 2 eggs, beaten with ½ cup of milk. Next dip the oysters in the egg and milk, then in cracker dust. Fry in hot lard.

MEATS.

"There's no want of meats, sir,
Portly and curious viands are prepared
To please all kinds of appetite."
—Massenger.

Beef, a la Mode.

4 pints of bread crumbs, as fine as possible; 2 large onions, chopped fine; 2 heaping teaspoonfuls of ground cloves. 2 of allspice; 2½ of black pepper, ¼ teaspoonful (scant measure) cayenne pepper, ½ small nutmeg, grated; not quite ½ pound butter, (make it over salty to taste, as the salt cooks out of the filling into the beef;) 2 eggs, ½ or ¾ pound fresh fat pork, 6 or 8 pounds beef of the tender part of the round. Place the bread crumbs in a large bowl; add both kinds of pepper, salt and spices. When well mixed, add onions and butter; last of all add the eggs. Mix the whole thoroughly with the hands. After the beef has been washed and pounded with an old-fashioned wooden potato masher, enough to make it more tender, though not to break it, wipe with a dry cloth and lay it on a board or waiter. Make slanting incisions into the beef with a long narrow knife. Into each separate incision run your finger, crook the end of it

and tear the centre of the beef so that the filling will spread nicely through the beef, at the same time taking care not to enlarge the opening near the top. Now the meat is ready for the filling. Of the latter, reserve $\frac{1}{4}$ to put over the top of the beef after it is boiled. Open an incision by running the finger in; then take a small portion of the filling, squeeze in the hand, and force it into the opening. After all the incisions are filled, lard each one with long ,narrow strips of the fat pork. Shape it nicely, running in skewers to keep it in position, and tie with string. Put in an iron pot to boil; nearly cover beef with cold water, mace and salt. Do not let it come to a boil too quickly, boil gently 6 or 7 hours, until it is tender enough to be lifted out without breaking. Put in a pan; take out skewers, and cut the strings. Put the rest of filling on top and sides; moisten with fat skimmed off of water it was boiled in. Bake in a moderate oven 1 or 2 hours, until all water it was boiled in is used in basting. After it has stood in the oven 10 minutes to harden the oftener it is basted the better. It is better to cook the day before using. Let it cool in pan it was baked in, as there is then less danger of being broken. Use baker's bread for filling. Cut the beef in very thin slices.

Meat Cakes with Tomato Sauce.

Take cold bits of meat of any kind; chop fine. To a pint of chopped meat add 1 egg, salt and pepper to season well, some chopped parsley, and a slice of bread that has been soaked in milk. Form into small cakes, dip in crumbs, and fry a nice brown in butter. For the sauce, stew half a can of tomatoes; mix smooth a tablespoonful each of butter and flour; strain the tomatoes into this and stir over the fire until it is the consistency of gravy. Pour over the meat cakes and serve at once.

Sweet Breads.

Mrs. John Weimer.

Scald and take off skins; soak in salted water $\frac{1}{2}$ hour; flour the pan and lay in the sweet-breads, piece of butter on each one; flour, pepper and salt them, and put into the oven. Do not put any water with them. Bake 20 minutes. Before taking out of the pan, add cream and a little flour.

Meat Pie.
Mrs. J. D. Keefer, Columbia.

You can take the meat of any kind left from the meal before; cut it up in small pieces, and add the dressing left to it with a little water. Put on the stove and boil a few minutes, then drain the meat from the dressing. Take a pudding dish, grease well, and put the meat in bottom. Then make the following batter and put on top of meat: 1 egg, 1 cup of flour, 1 cup of sweet milk, 1½ teaspoonfuls of baking powder. Beat well, then put on to top of meat and bake in hot oven. When done, cut in pieces to serve, and make a nice dressing out of the broth left from the meat, and pour on pie as you serve.

Scalloped Mutton.

Cut cold cooked mutton into small pieces. Put a layer of bread crumbs on the bottom of shallow dish, then layer of mutton, then brown sauce. Moisten some bread crumbs in melted butter; spread over the top. Bake until crumbs are brown. Other kinds of cold meat may be prepared same way.

Spiced Beef.
R. M. Brown.

3 pounds fresh beef, chopped very fine; 6 soda crackers, chopped very fine; 3 eggs, well beaten; butter, the size of an egg; 3 tablespoons of sweet milk, 1 tablespoon of salt, 1 teaspoon of pepper, 1 small onion. Press in a bread tin and bake 1½ hours slowly. Slice and eat cold.

Hamburg Steak.
H. M. M.

Take lean raw beef; chop fine. Add onions to taste, pepper and salt, and bind together with 1 egg. Make into small, flat cakes. Dip lightly in flour. Be sure to have pan hot; butter well; and fry quick, like beefsteak.

Baked Hash.
Mrs. Gingrich.

1 cup cold, chopped roast beef, a cup of boiled rice, cup of milk, 1 egg, 2 tablespoons butter, ¼ teaspoon salt, ⅛ teaspoon pepper. Put the milk over the fire in a saucepan, and when

hot, add all the other things except the egg. Stir 2 minutes; remove from the fire and add the egg, well beaten. Turn into a pudding dish, and bake 20 minutes.

Baked Hash.
Elizabeth Hammond Hoffer.

1 pound cooked meat, chopped fine. Boil ½ pint milk, with 2 tablespoonfuls of rolled crackers, 1 teaspoonful of flour, 1 teaspoonful of butter (if the meat is not rich). Add the meat, yolks of 2 eggs, parsley and seasoning. Put in a baking-dish. Stir in very lightly the beaten whites of 2 eggs. Bake ½ hour.

Veal Loaf.
Susan Houck.

3 pounds raw veal, chopped fine; 1 tablespoon of salt, 1 tablespoon of black pepper, 8 buttered crackers, pounded fine; 3 tablespoons of cream, 2 eggs, well beaten; butter, size of an egg; nutmeg. Mix all together. Form into a loaf, and bake 2 hours. If baked in a pan, baste with water and butter.

Veal Loaf.
Mrs. J. Dewald.

3 nice veal steaks, boiled. When cold, chop fine 5 lunch crackers or 10 small crackers; 3 eggs, well beaten; 1 small onion, cut fine. Mix all together, and season to taste with salt and pepper, 6 tablespoonfuls of broth, 1 tablespoonful of flour to make it into a loaf. Bake in the oven till brown, basting often. Slice thin, and eat when cold.

Veal Loaf.
Mrs. Coburn, Indianapolis, Ind.

2 pounds of veal, ½ pound pork, 1 dozen rolled crackers. 3 eggs, salt and pepper, ½ cup of milk. Bake little over an hour. Chop veal and pork fine. Nice hot and cold.

Saures-gedempfedes Rind-fleisch.
Mrs. J. C. Schmidt.

5 pounds beef, with little or no bone, very little fat. Put in a stone jar or crock; rub with salt, pepper, 1 teaspoon ground cloves, ½ teaspoon ground allspice; cover with vinegar; add ½ lemon (cut away white rind), 1 onion, 3 or 4 bay leaves. Turn every day. In winter, allow to stand a week; in warm weather,

2 or 3 days. Prepare like a pot roast, using the vinegar for a liquid, instead of water. Make a gravy, thickened with flour, using the vinegar.

Katuffel Glace to Eat with Saures Rind-fleisch.
Mrs. J. C. Schmidt.

Pare, boil potatoes, mash very fine, and then have 1 quart mashed potatoes; salt to taste. Mix 1 beaten egg, 3 tablespoons flour, well into potatoes (it must not stick to the fingers). Cut a cupful stale bread into cubes; fry brown in lard. Take a spoonful of potato mixture, flatten in your floured hand, put a few pieces of bread on top, fold it so as to make a round ball, drop it into a vessel of boiling water. Boil about 15 minutes, take out with a skimmer, arrange on a platter, garnish with the remaining bread cubes.

Dried Beef in Cream.

Shave your beef very fine, and pour over it boiling water a few minutes. Pour this off and put good rich cream or milk on and let come to a boil. If you use milk, thicken with a little flour. Season with pepper.

Frizzled Beef.

1 pound dried beef, sliced very thin. Freshen if too salt. 10 or 11 eggs. Melt some butter in a pan and put in the beef, torn fine, and eggs. Stir a very short time. Serve hot, immediately.

Baked Ham.

For a 20 pound ham, soaked over night. Next day scrape off the ragged edges, put in sufficient boiling water to cover. Boil it 2 hours. Let it remain in the water to cool. Take out, skin, and put it in the oven with a teacup of water. After it is warmed through, sprinkle a layer of white sugar, moistened with cider vinegar, in which a teaspoonful of ground mustard is mixed. Sprinkle with this mixture 5 times, until the sugar is $\frac{1}{2}$ inch thick. Bake 2 hours. Garnish with parsley and celery.

Snipes.
Mrs. M. R.

Snipe are best roasted with a piece of pork tied to the breast, or they may be stuffed and baked.

THERE IS BUT ONE FIRST CLASS....
JEWELRY STORE IN LEBANON....

 and that is **J. J. Cohn's**

J. C. SCHMIDT, Manager.

731 Cumberland Street...

**NEWNESS, GOODNESS, QUALITY,
ASSORTMENT AND PRICES**
Make it the BEST.

SPICES AND FLAVORING EXTRACTS.

In selecting our Spices we use the greatest care, and buy only from first-class houses. Our Flavoring Extracts are guaranteed to be superior preparations. The materials used in their manufacture are the best.

PERFUMES AND TOILET ARTICLES.

A full line of Perfumes and Toilet Articles in regular stock and always at the Lowest Prices.

DRUGS.

We pay particular attention to the quality and identity of our Drugs, and all Prescriptions are compounded with the greatest care and accuracy.

CENTRAL DRUG STORE,
FRANK H. ATKINS, PH. G.
26 N. EIGHTH STREET, LEBANON, PA.

VEGETABLES.
"Captus Nidore Culinoe."

Boston Baked Beans.

Wash 1 quart of marrowfat beans, boil until soft; take a piece of fresh pork, cut in small squares on the top; lay in a roasting pan, add one layer of beans, 2 tablespoonfuls of molasses, sprinkle with salt and pepper; add the remainder of the beans, then the molasses, salt and pepper. Bake in a moderate oven until a nice brown.

Creamed Potatoes.
Miss Ella Houseman.

1 pint cold boiled potatoes, cut in dice; 1 cup milk; butter size of an egg; 1 tablespoon of flour; pepper and salt. Add potatoes when it boils. Add a little dried celery.

Baked Tomatoes.

Take nice ripe tomatoes, cut off the top, take out pulp and juice. Put half a sliced onion into a saucepan with ½ teaspoon of butter, and let it fry. When nearly done, add the tomatoes, pepper and salt; in about 2 minutes a little soaked bread and chopped parsley. Then take a spoon and fill each tomato with this paste; dust them with bread crumbs, and put them in a pan and bake in the oven.

Corn Pudding.
Mrs. Jos Krause.

1 dozen ears of corn, cut off; 1 quart of sweet milk; 4 eggs, the whites beaten separately; add last butter, size of an egg, pepper and salt. Bake in a hot oven.

Asparagus.
Mrs. W. W. W.

Wash well; put on stove in boiling water; boil 5 minutes, pour off water, add more boiling hot, boil 10 to 15 minutes; then put in a lump of butter, salt and pepper (some stir in a thickening made of 1 teaspoon or flour mixed up with cold water); cut and toast 2 or 3 thin slices of bread, spread with butter, and put in a dish, and over them turn asparagus and gravy. The water must be boiled down until just enough for the gravy, which is made as above.

Scalloped Tomatoes.

Take tomatoes fully ripe; scald, remove the skins; cover the bottom of a buttered pudding dish with a layer of tomatoes; season with pepper and salt, cover with a layer of bread, buttered, and so alternately, until the dish is full, finishing at the top with the tomatoes. Bake in a moderate oven $\frac{1}{2}$ hour. Serve hot in the dish in which it was baked.

Browned Potatoes.

Mary E. Banks, Chambersburg, Pa.

Pare the potatoes, cut in pieces $1\frac{1}{2}$ inches square; put in cold water for $\frac{1}{2}$ hour; drain all the water off; put enough lard in the kettle to cover the potatoes. When lard is boiling hot (not before), put in the potatoes and cook until they are a delicate brown. Sweet potatoes cooked this way are delicious, sweet and mealy.

Potato Noodles.

Annie Hottenstein.

Grate 1 dozen boiled potatoes; add 2 eggs, a little salt, $\frac{1}{2}$ cup of milk, enough flour to knead stiff, then cut in small pieces; roll each piece long and round, 1 inch thick. Fry in plenty of lard and butter, or cottolene, to a nice brown.

Baked Potatoes.

Mrs. T. S. Walmer.

Take 6 large potatoes and bake them in the oven. When soft, cut in half and take out the inside; add onion, pepper, salt, parsley and butter. Mash well and add the beaten whites of 2 eggs. Put back in the shell again and brown in the oven.

Baked Sweet Potatoes.

Mary E. Banks, Chambersburg, Pa.

Boil the potatoes, slice lengthwise; put a layer of potatoes in a buttered dish, sprinkle with cinnamon and sugar; put tiny bits of butter here and there. Add another layer of potatoes;

sprinkle as before, and continue in same way until all is used, putting a little more butter on last layer. Bake in a good oven until a delicate brown, and serve.

Potato Cakes.
Mrs. W. G. Garverich.

2 cups of mashed potatoes, 1 cup of sweet milk, a little salt, flour enough to make them stiff enough to fry, a little baking powder and 2 eggs.

Boston Baked Beans.
Mrs. E. D. Burkett, New York.

1 pound of beans, 1 pound fresh pork, 1 onion (sliced), 1 tablespoon of mustard (dry), 4 tablespoons of syrup, pepper and salt. Put all together in a bean pot and bake in a hot oven 5 or 6 hours. Soak beans before using.

Creamed Onions.
Mrs. S. H. Reisner.

After peeling in a bowl of water, boil in plenty of salted water, and, unless the onions are very mild, change the water when parboiled. When very tender drain thoroughly. Make a cream sauce by rubbing together a tablespoonful of butter with one of flour and a pint of milk. Let the onions simmer gently in this sauce for a few minutes, and serve.

Left Over Stewed Tomatoes.

Boil two-thirds of a cup of rice in 2 cups water, adding $\frac{1}{2}$ teaspoonful of salt at the time you pour the boiling water on the rice. Cook until soft, which will be in $\frac{1}{2}$ or $\frac{3}{4}$ of an hour. Remove the cover and stir the rice carefully with a fork to let the steam escape and dry off the rice. Heat the tomatoes which were left, season them quite highly with salt and pepper (cayenne if you like); add to the rice a tablespoon of butter; stir in carefully, and when melted, pour over the tomatoes, and stir that also into the rice. Serve at once as a vegetable, and you will be surprised to find it so good.

Scalloped Potatoes.

Pare and slice the potatoes thin. Put some butter in the bottom of a baking dish, then a layer of potatoes, salt, pepper and butter. Continue this until the dish is full; sprinkle flour over the top and cover with milk. Bake an hour. Should be thick and creamy when done.

Baked Squash.

Cut in pieces, scrape well, and bake an hour or more. Scrape out and mash like potatoes. It is much dryer and better baked than boiled.

Corn Fritters.

1 pint grated corn, 3 eggs, 1 tablespoonful melted butter, ½ cup sweet milk, 1 cup flour. Fry in hot lard or bake on a griddle.

Corn Mock Oysters.

1 pint grated corn, 3 tablespoons milk, 1 teacupful flour, having a large spoonful of Cleveland baking powder; butter, size of an egg; 1 egg, salt and pepper. Fry in hot butter.

Parsnips.

Scrape and wash the parsnips and parboil. Take a baking dish and put in several pieces of butter. Place in the parsnips and bake until tender. Serve with melted butter or good beef gravy.

Parsnips are also nice parboiled and then fried brown.

Fried Tomatoes.

Cut green or solid ripe tomatoes across the tomato, season with salt and pepper, dip each slice in egg and cracker dust or flour. Fry in hot butter or lard. Equal to egg plant.

Macaroni.

Soak an hour or two in warm water. Then butter a baking dish, put in a layer of macaroni seasoned with pepper and salt, cover with fine crumbs, add another layer, and so on until the dish is full. Have crumbs on top. Cover with rich milk, season and lay small pieces of butter on top. Bake an hour. Cheese can be added if preferred.

VEGETABLES.

Baked Beans.

If, my dear Rural, you should ever wish
For breakfast or dinner a tempting dish
Of the beans so famous in Boston town,
You must read the rules I here lay down.
When the sun has set in golden light,
And around you fall the shades of night,
A large, deep dish you first prepare;
A quart of beans select with care;
And pick them over until you find
Not a speck or a mote is left behind.
A lot of cold water on them pour,
'Til every bean is covered o'er,
And they seem to your poetic eye
Like pearls in the depth of sea to lie;
Here, if you please, you may let them stay
Till after breakfast the very next day,
When a parboiling process must be gone through
(I mean for the beans, and not for you).
Then,if in the pantry, there still should be
That bean-pot, so famous in history,
With all due deference bring it out
And, if there's a skimmer lying about,
Skim half of the beans from the boiling pan
Into the bean pot as fast as you can;
Then turn to Biddy and calmly tell her
To take a huge knife and go to the cellar;
For you must have, like Shylock of old,
"A pound of flesh," ere your beans grow cold;
But very unlike that ancient Jew,
Nothing but pork will do for you.
Then tell at once your maiden fair,
In the choice of the piece to take great care,
For a streak of fat and a streak of lean
Will give the right flavor to every bean.
This you must wash and rinse, and score,
Put into the pot and around it pour

The rest, 'til the view presented seems
Like an island of pork in an ocean of beans;
Pour on boiling hot water enough to cover
The tops of the beans completely over,
Shove into the oven and bake till done,
And the triumph of Yankee cookery's won!

Aparagus.

Cook the asparagus (tied in bundles) in boiling salt water for 15 minutes. Drain, add a cup of cream or milk, let it boil, and season with salt, pepper, butter, and a litlte flour.

Dandelions.

Cut off the leaves, pick over carefully, wash, put in boiling water and boil half an hour. Drain, put in salted boiling water and cook until tender. Drain, season with salt, pepper, butter. Or they may be boiled with salt pork or corned beef.

Egg Plant.

Pare and slice thin. Make a batter with 1 egg, 1 tablespoon flour, ½ cup water, and salt. Dip each slice in the batter and fry brown in hot lard.

Sauer Kraut.

Take a boiling piece of beef and boil an hour. Then put in the kraut and boil together 2 hours. Add salt. 20 minutes before dinner, take 1 pint flour, 1 egg, 1½ teaspoonfuls Cleveland baking powder, a small piece of butter, and pour over slowly a little boiling water at a time—just to scald. Drop this with the meat and kraut. Cook a short time and serve.

Cream Cabbage.

Beat the yolks of 2 eggs, ½ cup sugar, ½ cup vinegar, butter size of an egg, salt and pepper, 1 teaspoonful mustard. Put the mixture into a saucepan and stir until it boils. Then stir in 1 cup sweet cream, let it boil, and pour over the cabbage hot. Or reserve the cream, whip, and pour over the cabbage last. Mix in a few celery seeds.

Scalloped Cabbage.

Cut the cabbage fine and boil a short time in salt and water.

Drain and put in a baking dish, season well, put bread crumbs and a little butter on top, and cover with rich milk. Bake until cabbage is well done. This is a very delicate and nice way to cook cabbage.

ENTREES.

"It is the bounty of nature that we live; but of philosophy that we live well."
—Seneca.

Salmon Croquettes.
Mrs. J. C. Schmidt.

Chop fine 1 can salmon, season with parsley, lemon juice, pepper and salt to taste. Put 1 cup cream over to boil; into 1 tablespoon butter rub 3 tablespoons flour; add slowly to boiling cream away from fire. Put over again; boil up while you stir quickly; then mix with salmon. Put away to cool; mould; dip in egg, then bread crumbs. Fry in lard, or butter and lard or cottolene.

Potato Croquettes.
Emma Richards.

2 cups of mashed potatoes, 2 tablespoonfuls of cream, 1 teaspoon onion juice, yolks of 2 eggs, 1 tablespoon chopped parsley, butter size of a walnut, a sprinkle of nutmeg and cayenne pepper, salt to suit the taste; beat the yolks until light and add to the potatoes; then add all the other ingredients; mix, put in a kettle and stir over the fire until the mixture leaves the sides of the kettle; when cool, form into any shape desired. Roll in egg, then in cracker dust or bread crumbs, and fry. This will make 12 croquettes.

Potato Croquettes.

Pare and boil ¼ peck of potatoes; when done, mash till smooth; peel and slice 2 large onions and fry (slightly) in ¼ pound butter; add this to the mashed potatoes, 3 eggs, a sprig of parsley, and salt. Mold into croquettes and fry in hot lard or cottolene.

ENTREES.

Potato Croquettes.
Mrs. Roby.

Take 12 large potatoes, boil until done; then mash through a colander; add ¼ pound of butter, a small onion and a teaspoonful of parsley, both chopped fine; pepper, salt and a pinch of ground mace; 2 eggs beaten lightly; beat all well together, and if not soft enough, add a little cream or milk. Mould into croquette form or into ball form, just as preferred; dip in eggs and bread crumbs, and fry in boiling lard. They are better if made up several hours before cooking and laid away in the ice chest to harden.

Salmon Croquettes.
Mrs. Julia A. Strider, Cincinnati, O.

1 can salmon, remove bones and skins; 3 boiled potatoes, mashed; 2 eggs, salt to taste, 1 teaspoonful of butter, ½ teaspoonful mustard, pepper and salt to taste. Mix thoroughly and mould. Roll in egg and cracker crumbs, and fry in hot lard or cottolene.

Oyster Omelet.
Mrs. T. B. Johnson, Tuscumbia.

Add to ½ cup of cream 6 eggs, beaten very light; season with pepper and salt, and pour into a frying-pan with a tablespoon of butter; drop in a dozen large oysters, cut in halves or chopped fine, with parsley, and fry until a light brown. Double it over and serve immediately.

Salmon Gratin.
Mrs. John C. Urich, Marquette, Mich.

1 coffee cup cold boiled salmon, pulled into flakes with silver fork; mix with this ½ cup cold drawn butter; pepper and salt; fill small shells with mixture, cover with cracker crumbs, and brown in oven.

Chicken Croquettes.
Mrs. J. H. Roberts.

1 pint of chicken, minced fine; add salt, pepper, parsley, ¼ cup of butter; mix well together; moisten with milk or half cream, if you have it; mould and dip in beaten egg; then roll in bread crumbs or cracker dust; drain on brown paper. Veal and beef can be prepared in the same way.

ENTREES.

Chicken Croquettes.
Mrs. Foster.

1½ cups chopped chicken, 2 tablespoons butter, 2 tablespoons corn starch, 1 pint hot milk, 1 teaspoonful parsley, 1 teaspoonful salt and pepper; flavor with onion juice.

Cod Fish Balls.
Mrs. P. O'Neil.

Soak codfish, cut in pieces, 1 hour in lukewarm water; remove skin and bones, pick in small pieces; return to stove in cold water. As soon as it begins to boil, change the water and bring to boil again. Have ready, potatoes boiled tender, well mashed and seasoned with butter. Mix thoroughly with the potatoes half the quantity of the codfish, while both are still hot. Form into flat, thick cakes or round balls; fry in hot lard or drippings, or dip in hot fat like doughnuts. The addition of a beaten egg before making into balls renders them lighter. Cold potatoes may be used by re-heating, adding a little cream and butter, and mixing while hot.

Cod Fish Balls.
Esther Helms.

Take codfish, 1 pound; boil and shred; take 2 pounds potatoes, boil and mash; add 2 eggs, 1 cup of milk, and a lump of butter the size of an egg; add fish; fry in butter or lard or cottolene, and serve hot.

Meat Croquettes.
Mrs. J. D. Keefer, Columbia.

2 cups of mashed potatoes; 1 egg; beat with potatoes, about 1 cup of bread crumbs, and 1 cup of meat, chopped fine; mix well together; then shape them in a medium size spoon and drop in hot lard so they can swim; fry to a nice brown.

Cold Meat Croquettes.

1 pint of cold chopped meat; ½ pint of milk; salt and pepper to taste; 1 tablespoon of butter, 2 of flour, 1 of onion juice, and a little parsley. Mix butter and flour together, add the boiling milk, stir until it thickens and pour over the meat. When cool, form into balls and fry in lard or cottolene.

Veal Croquettes.

R. M. Brown.

Boil 3 pounds of veal with a little salt and a small onion; when tender, mince fine; mince another onion and parsley and 1 ounce of butter; put in a pan with ½ teacup of flour; make it a light brown; then add a teacup of the soup or stock, having skimmed the fat; stir until a smooth paste; pepper and salt to taste, a little nutmeg, juice of 1 lemon; mix well, then mould into croquettes; dip in egg and cracker dust or bread crumbs. Fry in boiling lard or cottolene.

Croquettes.

Cut fine as mince meat, beef, or veal, or chicken enough to fill a good sized tincup; put into a saucepan and nearly cover with water; take butter, size of a walnut, rub into a large tablespoon of flour; add to the meat, then add ½ cup cream; season with sweet marjoram and sage; let it cool, take a tablespoon and shape into longish rolls; dip in egg and cracker dust and fry in hot lard like oysters.

McNEAL'S DENTAL PARLORS,

DENTAL OPERATIONS WITH NEATNESS AND DISPATCH.

120 NORTH 8TH ST., LEBANON, PA.

A Good Set of Teeth, . . $5.00	Teeth Extracted, ... 25c
Best Set of Teeth, . . . $8.00	Vitalized Air, ... 50c
Partial Sets, . . . $2.00 and up	Gold Crowns, . . $5.00 to $8.50
Gold Fillings, . . $1.00 and up	Porcelain Crowns, "white," $4.00
Teeth Cleaned, ... 75c	Bridge Work, . . $6.00 per tooth

Silver or Amalgam Fillings, 75c and 50c
Broken Plates Repaired, $1.00 and up

EXAMINATION FREE.   CONSULATION FREE.
ALL WORK GUARANTEED.   EXAMINE OUR WORK.

CONSULT US AND YOU WILL SAVE MONEY.

All work guaranteed equal to any in this or any other city.

SALADS.

"To make a perfect salad there should be a spendthrift for oil, a miser for vinegar, a wise man for salt, and a madcap to stir the ingredients up and mix them well together."—Spanish Proverb.

Nut Salad.
R. D. Smith.

Take half as many picked walnuts, pecans or butternuts as you have chopped celery; mix with mayonnaise dressing and serve on lettuce leaves.

Chicken Salad.
Mrs. S. Ogden.

Chop fine 1 chicken, cooked tender; 1 head of cabbage and 5 cold hard-boiled eggs; season with salt, pepper and mustard to taste; warm 1 pint vinegar; add half a teacup butter; stir until melted; pour hot over the mixture; stir thoroughly and set away to cool.

Salad Dressing.
Mrs. D. M. Karmany.

2 raw eggs; 1 tablespoonful of butter; 8 large tablespoonfuls good vinegar; salt, pepper and sugar to taste. Put in a dish over boiling water, stirring until it becomes thick like cream.

Orange Salad.
Mrs. T. Fosbinner.

Take 1 dozen oranges, peel and cut in slices; lay a layer of them in a dish; sprinkle over each layer, so as to cover, prepared cocoanut, and squeeze the juice of 3 oranges on top.

Salad Dressing.

1 egg; butter size of a walnut; 4 tablespoons sweet cream; 4 tablespoons vinegar; ½ teaspoon prepared mustard; season to taste and boil till thick.

Salad Dressing.
Mrs. J. H. Roberts.

1 cup of vinegar; 1 beaten egg; 1 teaspoon of flour; 1 teaspoon of ground mustard; cayenne pepper, salt and sugar.

SALADS.

Tomato and Lettuce Salad.
Mrs. Dr. A. J. Riegel.

Pick out crisp lettuce leaves; lay a raw tomato, peeled and cut in half, on each leaf; arrange on a platter. In serving, pour mayonnaise dressing over the tomato.

Potato Salad.
Mrs. J. Marshall Funck.

3 large potatoes boiled, and sliced when cold; 1 large onion, grated; 1 stalk of celery, cut in fine pieces; mix well together. The dressing: Yolk of 1 egg, teaspoonful of mustard, teaspoonful of sugar, $\frac{1}{2}$ cup of sour cream, $\frac{1}{2}$ cup of vinegar, salt to suit the taste. Take a piece of bacon, cut it in small pieces, and then fry it nice and brown; pour dressing on bacon and boil until thick, and then pour on potatoes while hot.

Brown Sauce.

Melt and brown 1 tablespoon of butter; add 1 tablespoonful of flour, and cook 2 minutes; add gradually 1 cup of mutton broth (1 cup of hot water may be used), and cook until it thickens and boils; add $\frac{1}{2}$ teaspoon of salt, 1 teaspoon Worcestershire sauce or catsup, 1 teaspoon of chopped onion.

Cold Cream Sauce.

Stir to a cream, 1 cupful of sugar; $\frac{1}{2}$ cup butter; then add a cupful of sweet thick cold cream; flavor to taste; stir well, and set it in a cool place.

Delmonico Dressing.
Mrs. T. S. Walmer.

Cream well 1 tablespoon of butter; yolks of two eggs (raw); 1 small tablespoon mustard; $\frac{1}{4}$ teaspoon salt; 2 tablespoons of sugar; a dash of pepper; $\frac{1}{2}$ cup of vinegar, and last of all $\frac{1}{2}$ cup cream. Let come to a boil, and then set away to get cold.

Chicken Salad.
Mrs. Frank Pratt.

Cut fine 4 or 5 heads of white bunch celery; place in a glass or white china dish; mince all the white meat of a boiled or stewed fowl, without the skin and put with the celery. Rub the yolks of 2 hard-boiled eggs to a smooth paste with a dessert spoonful of melted butter; add to it 2 teaspoonfuls of prepared mustard and a small teaspoonful of white sugar, and put it to it, gradually stirring it in a large cup of strong vinegar. Do not pour the dressing over the chicken until ready to serve. White heart lettuce may be used instead of celery.

Chicken Salad Dressing.
Mrs C. D. Mish.

3 raw eggs, well beaten; 6 tablespoonfuls of cream; 2 tablespoonfuls mixed mustard; 2 tablespoonfuls melted butter; 4 tablespoonfuls vinegar; salt and cayenne pepper to taste. Boil to the thickness of cream; let cool before using.

Potato Salad.
H. M. M.

6 boiled potatoes; 3 hard-boiled eggs; 1 raw onion. Dressing: 1 egg, ½ cup of vinegar; ½ cup of water; 2 tablespoons cream; 1 tablespoon sugar; 1 tablespoon mustard; 1 tablespoon of oil or butter; pinch of salt.

Hot Potato Salad.

Boil potatoes in their skins; when done, peel and slice. Make a dressing of 1 tablespoon flour; 1 egg; ½ teaspoon sugar; a pinch of salt, pepper; equal quantities of milk or sour cream and vinegar. Boil this dressing in a skillet, in which bacon, cut in small squares, and sliced onions have been fried; pour over the potatoes.

Potato Salad.
Mrs. H. Yeamen.

Slice cold boiled potatoes very thin; place in a dish, stewing among them pepper and salt and a little onion and parsley, chopped fine; enough vinegar to moisten. Make the salad an hour or two before it is to be eaten.

Chicken Salad.

The white meat of 1 boiled chicken; three-fourths as much of celery; 2 hard-boiled eggs; 1 raw egg, well beaten; 1 teaspoonful of salt; 1 teaspoonful of pepper; 1 teaspoonful of mustard; 3 tablespoons of melted butter; 2 tablespoons of white sugar; ½ cup of vinegar.

Cream Dressing for Cold Slaw.
Miss Laura Sharp, Kingston.

2 tablespoons whipped sweet cream; 2 of sugar, and 4 of vinegar; beat well and pour over cabbage previously cut very fine and seasoned with salt.

Chicken Salad.
Mrs. J. E. M.

4 pounds of chicken will make a salad for 10 or 12 persons. Cut the light and dark meat into fine pieces with a sharp knife; use two-thirds chicken to one-third celery, cut fine; mix the salad with the dressing; save enough to pour over top 1 hour before serving.

Salmon Salad.

1 can of salmon; $1\frac{1}{2}$ cups of chopped celery or lettuce; salt, pepper and mustard to taste. Stir the above into 1 cup of boiling vinegar; then stir in 2 beaten eggs; add a tablespoonful of butter. When cool, pour over salmon and lettuce, and mix thoroughly.

Salad Dressing.
Mrs. John C. Urich, Marquette, Mich.

Yolks of 4 eggs; 4 tablespoons melted butter; 2 teaspoons mustard; 1 saltspoon pepper; 1 teaspoon salt; 1 cup cream to be heated. When hot, pour in the former mixture, stir constantly until thick; when ready to use, thin with vinegar.

Salad Dressing.
Miss Hettie Kendall.

Break 1 egg in a bowl; add $\frac{1}{2}$ teaspoon salt and 1 teaspoon sugar; beat well together with two-thirds cup vinegar and water. Put butter, the size of a walnut, in a pan; let it brown the least bit over the fire. Pour in the dressing, let it boil up, then pour over the salad and serve.

Mayonnaise Dressing.
Mrs. Annie Koch, Pottsville.

Yolks of 4 eggs; $\frac{1}{2}$ teaspoon of salt (small); $\frac{1}{2}$ teaspoon of sugar; 2 teaspoons of made mustard; pinch of red pepper; vinegar to taste. Put this in a bowl, put the bowl in a kettle of boiling water, and stir constantly until it thickens. Thin this

SALADS.

with cream or milk. When the latter is used, a tablespoon of butter must be used before boiling.

Celery Salad.
Mrs. Chance.

Take 1 stalk of celery, 1 apple and 1 onion; chop all very fine, and season with salt, pepper, sugar and vinegar; add sweet cream to make it tasty.

Salad Dressing.
M. A. McFarland.

About 2 even tablespoonfuls dry mustard; 1 teaspoonful salt; 1 teaspoonful sugar; scald with hot water enough to mix; 3 eggs; ½ cup vinegar; two-thirds cup milk, and bring to a full boil.

Salmon Turbet Dressing.

1 pint milk; 3 teaspoons flour; boil the milk and thicken with flour; then add ½ cup butter. When this is cool, add 2 eggs, beaten together. Use a baking dish and put a layer of salmon, salt, red and black pepper, and a layer of dressing covered with bread crumbs. Bake ½ hour. 1 can of salmon without the liquid.

Fish Salad.

Take a fresh white fish or trout; boil and chop it, not too fine; put with the same quantity of chopped cabbage, celery or lettuce; season the same as chicken salad. Garnish with the tender leaves of the heart of lettuce.

Courbillon (Creole).
R. D. Smith.

Cut up into squares, any good frying fish; fry to a nice brown in cracker crumbs. Take 3 large tomatoes, 1 large sweet pepper, 1 onion, parsley, thyme, and sweet marjoram; chop all together, and steam until thoroughly tender; add butter, pepper and salt to taste. Boil until the consistency of sauce, and pour over the fish, very hot.

Lobster Salad.

1 can of lobster; 3 large bunches of celery; 2 tablespoonfuls of melted butter; 4 hard-boiled eggs, cut fine; add red and

black pepper, mustard and salt to taste; add 1 raw egg, well beaten; mix each article separately with a wooden spoon; add vinegar and whites of eggs, chopped fine.

Veal Salad.
R. M. Brown.

Boil veal until tender; cut into dice; use equal parts veal and celery. Now prepare the dressing. Take 3 eggs, beaten until well mixed; 2 tablespoonfuls of ground mustard; mix smooth, 3 spoonfuls of melted butter or olive oil, teaspoonful of sugar, 1 cup of cider vinegar; at the last 1 cup of sweet milk. Boil 5 minutes, stirring constantly. When it thickens, take from the fire and cool; salt and pepper to taste; mix, and garnish with celery tops.

Potato Salad Dressing.
Mrs. A. G. Banks, Middletown.

1 egg; butter, size of an egg; 6 tablespoonfuls of sweet cream; 2 teaspoonfuls sugar; 1 teaspoonful mustard, with vinegar enough to dissolve it; 6 tablespoonfuls vinegar; pepper and salt to taste. Beat egg in a bowl, add melted butter; then mustard, sugar, pepper, salt and vinegar; ¼ teaspoonful cayenne pepper. Boil in a dish over boiling water until thick; then add cream.

Salad Dressing.
Mrs. J. E. M.

1 tablespoon mustard; 1 tablespoon sugar; 1 teaspoon salt; 1 cup cream; 1 cup vinegar; 3 eggs. Mix sugar, salt and mustard together; add vinegar and eggs, well beaten; pour cream in slowly, stirring all the time; set in a dish of cold water and cook as soft as custard. When done, add a piece of butter as large as an egg and stir it thoroughly. Garnish with pieces of hard-boiled eggs and celery leaves.

OMELETS AND TOASTS.

Bread Omelet.
Sarah T. Paul.

Cut a slice of stale bread an inch thick; toast brown on both sides; lay it on a hot plate; sprinkle it with salt, and pour over it ½ cup of rich cream, and serve quickly.

Bread Omelet.

3 eggs; ½ cup bread crumbs; ¼ teaspoon salt; ½ cup of milk; sprinkle of pepper; butter. Beat the yolks of the eggs; add salt, pepper, milk and bread crumbs. Beat the whites of the eggs very stiff and cut them into the mixture. Put enough butter into an omelet pan to cover the bottom, when melted. Turn in the omelet, cook until firm, dry a few minutes in the oven and turn, after folding, upon a warm plate. Serve immediately.

Bread Omelet.
Maze Johnson.

Put into a stew pan a teacupful of bread crumbs; 1 cupful of cream or milk; a tablespoonful of butter; a sprinkle of salt and pepper. When the bread has absorbed the milk, pour in 4 or 5 eggs, beaten very light; beat all together a little more, and fry like plain omelet.

Egg Omelet.

6 eggs, whites and yolks beaten separately; ½ pint milk; 6 teaspoons corn starch; 1 teaspoon powder; a little salt. Add whites last; cook in butter.

Veal Omelet.
H. M. M.

3 pounds of veal; 6 soda crackers; 3 eggs; 2 teaspoonfuls of cream; salt, pepper and sweet marjoram. Make in a loaf, and bake 1 hour.

Beef Steak Toast.

Mrs. John Gortner, Goshen, Ind.

Chop cold steak very fine; cook in a little water, put in cream or milk; thicken; season with butter, salt and pepper, and pour it over slices of toast. Prepare boiled ham in the same way, adding the yolk of an egg.

Cheese Toast.

Toast thin slices of bread an even crisp brown; place on a warm plate, allowing one small slice to each person, and pour on enough melted cheese to cover them. Rich new cheese is best. Serve while warm. Many prefer a little prepared mustard spread over the toast before putting on the cheese.

Queen Esther's Toast.

Mrs. Geo. Kochenour.

A quart of new milk; 3 eggs. Mix $\frac{1}{4}$ cup of butter and $\frac{1}{2}$ cup of sugar to a cream; add the white of 1 egg, beaten stiff; put in a dish and set in a cold place to harden. This is called the hard sauce. Then take the milk and the 2 whole eggs, and the 1 yolk, and beat together; then take a loaf of Vienna bread and cut in pieces $1\frac{1}{2}$ inches thick; lay on a flat dish or pan and pour the custard over it. It takes almost 2 hours to absorb all the custard. I take about 11 pieces of bread, and it just takes it all nicely. You do not fry your bread until you are ready to serve it, as it must be eaten warm. Grease your skillet with butter instead of lard; then take your cake turner and lift your bread into the skillet, and fry a light brown, and serve with a spoonful of the hard sauce on top. Flavor the hard sauce with a spoonful of vanilla.

BOMGARDNER & CILLEY

...DEALERS IN...

Boots, Shoes, Trunks and Satchels

16 N. NINTH ST.
...Lebanon, Pa.

PUDDINGS.

"The proof of the pudding is in the eating."

Plum Pudding Sauce.
Mrs. Foster.

Take 1 cup sugar, $\frac{1}{2}$ cup butter, one spoonful flour; beat together till light and smooth; add pint boiling water; flavor with lemon.

(Creamy Sauce.)

Cream $\frac{1}{4}$ cup butter and add gradually $\frac{1}{2}$ cup sugar, 2 tablespoons milk; flavor with vanilla.

Cottage Pudding.
Mrs. Geo. Stanley.

1 pint of flour, 1 egg, 3 tablespoons of butter, 1 cup of sugar, 1 cup of sweet milk, 3 teaspoons of Cleveland baking powder. Bake 20 minutes in shallow pans; season to taste.

Bread Pudding.
Mrs. J. E. M.

3 slices stale bread, soaked in milk; when soft, mix 3 eggs and $\frac{1}{2}$ cup sugar; butter, size of 2 eggs; $\frac{1}{2}$ cup raisins; flavor with cinnamon. Bake until brown.

Steam Plum Pudding.

1 cup of molasses, 1 cup of chopped pork or a piece of butter, 1 cup of raisins, 1 cup of citron, 1 cup of milk, 2 cups of sifted flour, 1 teaspoonful of all kinds of spices except cloves; $\frac{1}{2}$ teaspoonful of soda; salt to suit taste; steam 3 hours.

Fruit Pudding.

1 cup of molasses, 1 cup of butter, 3 cups of flour, 2 teaspoons of Cleveland baking powder, 1 cup of milk, $\frac{1}{2}$ pound of raisins, $\frac{1}{2}$ pound of currants; cloves, nutmeg and cinnamon. Boil 3 hours and serve with cold sauce.

(Sauce for same.)

Beat to a cream $\frac{1}{2}$ cupful of butter and 1 cupful of fine white sugar; stir in the juice and grated rind of 1 lemon.

Orange Pudding.
Mrs. J. H. Roberts.

Slice 2 oranges, well sugared, in a glass dish; 1 pint of sweet milk, yolks of 4 eggs and the whites of 2, 1 tablespoonful corn starch, boiled; then pour over oranges. Just before using beat the whites of 2 eggs, place on top and sprinkle with sugar.

Honey Crumb Pudding
Miss McLaine.

2 cups flour, 1 cup molasses, 1½ cups milk, 1 cup sugar, 2 eggs, 2 tablespoons of butter, 2 teaspoons of soda, dissolved in hot water. Bake 1 hour. Serve with hard sauce.

(Sauce for same.)

1 cup of sugar, 1 egg, ½ cup of butter, 1 tablespoon of flour, 1 cup of hot water. Let it all cook up together.

Apple Pudding.
Mrs. S. E. Breslin.

Peel and slice 4 large apples. First place a layer of apples in dish, then a layer of bread crumbs. Beat 3 eggs in 1 pint of milk, 1 teaspoon of cinnamon; sweeten to taste; pour over the apples and bread crumbs. Bake until brown.

Christmas Plum Pudding.
Mrs. C. Shiner.

Chop very fine 1 pound candied orange and lemon peel, mixed; ½ pound citron, ½ ounce butter almonds, ½ pound beef suet, having removed the skin and fibre; add 1 pound brown sugar, ½ pound bread crumbs.

Plum Pudding.
Mrs. D. Hammond.

3 cups flour, 1 cup milk, 1 cup molasses, 1 cup chopped suet, 1 cup raisins, 1 cup currants, 1 tablespoonful of ground cinnamon, same of cloves, 2 teaspoonfuls of salt, 2 teaspoonfuls of soda dissolved in the milk; mix well together, tie it loosely and boil steadily for 3 hours.

Bread Pudding.
Mrs. Rev. I. C. Fisher.

1 cup of dried bread crumbs, put in baking dish and drop on pieces of butter. Make a custard of the yolks of 3 eggs, 1 cup

of sugar and 1 pint of milk; pour over the bread crumbs and bake. When done spread with currant jelly and the whites beaten stiff. Brown in oven.

Brown Getty.
Mrs. James Watson.

Grease a pudding dish and place in the bottom a layer of bread crumbs, then fill the dish with alternate layers of bread crumbs and sliced apples, strewing brown sugar, cinnamon and a little butter over each layer, topping off with crumbs. Bake 1 hour and serve with sauce.

Lemon Pudding.
Elizabeth Hammond Hoffer.

3 eggs, 1 pint of milk, butter, size of an egg; 2 handfuls of flour, 2 tablespoonfuls of sugar, 1 lemon. Boil butter, flour and milk until smooth; let stand until almost cold, add yolks of eggs, rind and juice of lemon, then the beaten whites. Bake in moderate oven 20 minutets.

Fruit Pudding.
Manda Hottenstein.

Sift together 1 quart flour, 3 teaspoons of Cleveland baking powder, $\frac{1}{2}$ teaspoon salt, 2 tablespoons of lard mixed in the flour; mix with cold water, roll out and spread the fruit on the dough, then roll together and boil $1\frac{1}{2}$ hours.

Cottage Pudding.
Amelia Ohlwiler, Altoona.

1 cup sugar, good $\frac{1}{2}$ cup butter, 2 eggs, $\frac{3}{4}$ cup sweet milk, 2 cups flour, 1 teaspoon baking powder. Bake and eat warm with lemon dressing.

(Sauce for same.)

Can be used with Cottage Pudding, Graham Pudding and Suet Pudding. 1 pint boiling water, 1 tablespoon corn starch, mixed smooth in cold water; a lump of butter, the juice and rind of 1 lemon, sugar to sweeten.

Old Fashioned Rice Pudding.

$\frac{1}{2}$ cup rice, 3 pints of milk, handful of raisins, sugar to taste; grated nutmeg on top; then put in oven and bake.

Rice Pudding.
Miss Hettie Kendall.

Boil in water ½ cup of rice; when done, add a quart of milk; leave it come to a boil, separate the yolks and whites of 2 eggs, beat the yolks and stir in the rice; sweeten it to taste; let boil again, take off the fire and stir in the whites of the eggs, beaten stiff. Flavor to taste. To be eaten cold.

Rice Pudding.
Mrs. James Watson.

1 quart milk, ½ teacup rice, 1 cup sugar. Bake slowly 2 hours or more. It should be cream like when done. A good test is to tip dish, if rice and milk move together it is done; if not sufficiently cooked the milk runs; if neither move it is done too much.

(Sauce for same.)

½ pint of milk, 1 tablespoonful of butter, 2 tablespoons of sugar, 1 tablespoon of flour, and 2 tablespoons of molasses. Boil 10 minutes.

Queen's Pudding.
Miss Tillie Follweiler.

1 pint of bread crumbs, 1 quart of milk, warmed and poured over the crumbs; yolks of 4 eggs well beaten with 1 cup of sugar and 1 teaspoon of butter. When baked spread over the top a layer of jelly or preserves. Beat the whites of the eggs and add 2 tablespoons of sugar and spread over the top; bake a light brown; serve warm, with sauce, or cold, with sugar and cream.

Tapioca Pudding.
Elma A. Fry, Pleasant Grove.

4 tablespoons of tapioca, 1 quart sweet milk, 4 eggs, 1 small piece of butter; sugar and vanilla to taste. Soak tapioca in milk.

Rice Pudding.
Mrs. Ira Rutter.

1 quart milk, 4 large tablespoons of rice; sweeten to taste; a small piece of butter; flavor with nutmeg; add a handful of raisins if liked. Boil all together till the rice is done, then brown in a quick oven.

Cocoanut Pudding.
Mrs. Southam.

1 cocoanut, grated; 1 pint of milk, ½ cup sugar, 3 eggs, 1 teaspoon of vanilla. Mix together and bake 30 minutes.

Cinderella Pudding.

1 quart of sweet milk, 5 eggs, 3 tablespoons of corn starch, 1 lemon, grated; sugar to taste; whites of eggs beaten stiff and sweetened, to be put on last, and put in oven to brown.

Queen Victoria's Favorite Pudding.

1 small box gelatine, dissolved in ½ pint of cold water, then add 1 pint boiling water, and at the same time 2 cups sugar and the juice of 2 lemons; also 2 banannas, 2 oranges, 6 figs and 10 English walnuts. Serve with cream.

Berry Pudding.
Mrs. Crowther.

2 eggs, 1½ cups sugar, 1 of sweet milk, 2 teaspoons baking powder, 1 pint flour and a little salt; add berries; to be eaten with milk. Bake in pudding pan.

Illinois Pudding.

Steam for ½ hour 1 egg, ¼ cup sugar, ½ cup butter, 1 cup sweet milk, 1 cup fruit (fresh or dried), 1 2-3 cups flour, 1 tablespoon baking powder.

Suet Pudding.
Amelia Ohlwiler, Altoona.

1 cup suet (shaved down fine), 2 cups flour, 2-3 cup sweet milk, ½ cup sugar, 3 eggs, a little salt, 1 cup raisins, 1 cup currants, 3 teaspoons baking powder; flavor with nutmeg; steam 2½ hours. For Lemon Dressing, see Dressings.

Graham Pudding.
Amelia Ohlwiler, Altoona.

1½ cups graham flour, ½ cup molasses, ¼ cup melted butter, ½ cup sweet milk, 1 egg, an even teaspoon soda, a little salt, ½ cup raisins, ½ cup currants; cinnamon, cloves and nutmeg. Steam 2½ hours. For Lemon Dressing, see Dressings.

Apple Pudding.
Mrs. James Watson.

Fill a buttered baking dish with sliced apples and pour over the top a batter made of 1 tablespoonful of butter, $\frac{1}{2}$ cup of sugar, 1 egg, $\frac{1}{2}$ cup of sweet milk, and 1 cup of flour, in which has been sifted 1 teaspoon of baking powder. Bake in a moderate oven till brown. Serve with cream and sugar or liquid sauce.

Rice Pudding Without Eggs.

To 1 quart of milk add 2 tablespoonfuls of rice, a pinch of salt, and sugar to suit the taste; put in a pudding dish and bake in a slow oven.

Apple Pudding.
Esther Helms.

Line pan with pastry; 1 pint of chipped apples, 1 ounce butter, 1 teaspoon cinnamon, 1 cup bread crumbs. Bake in oven.

Charlotte Russe Pudding.
Mrs. S. P. Newhard, Philadelphia.

1 quart milk, yolks of 4 eggs, 1 tablespoon sugar in the milk, 3 tablespoons flour; boil the milk; stir in the yolk (well beaten), then put in the flour or corn starch; flavor with vanilla. First layer of pudding, then cake (sponge cake is preferable), and so on; then beat the whites of the eggs to a stiff froth with a little sugar, and after the pudding is cooled a little, drop this on and put into the oven for a short time.

Snow Pudding.
Mrs. H. T. Atkins.

Cover $\frac{1}{2}$ box gelatine with cold water; let stand $\frac{1}{2}$ hour; put to this a pint of boiling water and 1 pound of sugar; stir until dissolved; squeeze in the juice of 3 lemons and strain into a dish; set on ice till cold. When thick, beat with an egg-beater until white; whip the whites of 3 eggs and stir into the pudding. Turn into a dish and stand in a cold place.

(Sauce for same.)

Beat the yolks of 3 eggs with $\frac{1}{2}$ cupful of sugar and a good pint of milk; stir over the fire until thick; flavor with vanilla. Serve cold with the pudding.

Apple Pudding.
Mrs. D. M. Karmany.

1 pint of flour, sifted, with 1½ teaspoonfuls of baking powder, 1 scant cup of sweet milk, ¼ cup of butter, pinch of salt, 1 egg, a few apples cut in slices over the top; sprinkle with sugar. Bake from 20 to 30 minutes.

Snow Pudding.
Mrs. D. M. Karmany.

½ package of gelatine, soaked in ½ cup of cold water 10 minutes; add 1 pint boiling water, 1 cup sugar; flavor with lemon or vanilla; when dissolved, strain and cool. Beat the whites of 3 eggs stiff and add to the mixture, which ought to be like soft jelly; beat together 5 minutes, then put into small moulds, enough for each person.

(Custard for same.)

1 pint of sweet milk, the yolks of 3 eggs, ½ cup of sugar, 1 teaspoon of corn starch. Flavor to taste.

Apple Snow Pudding.
Mrs Chas. H. Rockel, Allentown.

2 eggs, 2 apples (beat whites of eggs and grated apples together), pint sweet milk, sugar to taste; yolks of eggs and a little corn starch; boil like custard and pour it over grated apples and eggs.

Snow Pudding.
Mrs. J. Billingham.

Pour 1 pint of boiling water on ½ box of gelatine; add the juice and rind of 2 lemons and 2 cup of sugar; strain when cool and when it begins to congeal add the whites of 4 eggs that have been beaten to a stiff froth. Then beat the whole well together until quite stiff and put in mould.

Snow Pudding.
Laura Dewald.

½ box gelatine, 2 cups of sugar, 4 eggs, juice of 3 lemons, 1 quart of milk, 1 teaspoonful of vanilla, 1 pint of boiling water. Cover the gelatine with cold water and let it soak a ½ hour, then pour over it the boiling water; add the sugar, stir until it is dissolved, then add the juice and strain the whole into a tin basin; place this in a pan of ice water and let it stand until cold. When cold, beat with an egg beater until as white as snow; beat the whites of the eggs to a stiff froth and stir it into the pudding. Dip a fancy mould into cold water, turn the pudding into it and stand in a cold place 4 hours to harden.

Snow Pudding.
Mrs. Walter Randall.

1 pint of milk, 2 tablespoons of corn starch, whites of 3 eggs; dissolve the corn starch in a little of the milk, stir the sugar in the remainder of the milk, which place on the fire. When this begins to boil stir in the corn starch; stir constantly for a few minutes, when it will become a smooth paste. Now stir in the whites of the eggs, beaten to a stiff froth, and let it remain a little longer to cook the eggs. Flavor to taste. Mould and serve cold, with boiled custard, made of the yolks of the eggs, a pint of milk, and a scant ½ cup of sugar.

Snow Pudding.
Mrs. S. G. Valentine.

½ box Cox gelatine, ½ pound sugar (granulated), 2 lemons, 3 eggs, 1½ pints water, 1 pint milk. Slice the lemons and add the gelatine. Pour ½ pint cold water over it and let it stand 1 hour; then add sugar and 1 pint boiling water; strain, and when beginning to harden add the beaten whites of the eggs. Make a custard of the 3 yolks and 1 pint of milk. Flavor and sweeten to taste.

English Plum Pudding.
Mrs. Powick, Wilmington, Del.

1 pound seedless raisins, 1 pound currants, 2 ounces lemon peel, 1 teacup bread crumbs, 1 coffee cup fine chopped apples, 1 pound suet, 1½ pounds flour, 1 pound good brown sugar, 4 eggs, 1 nutmeg; mace, allspice, ground cloves and cinnamon, a little of each. Mix together in a stiff batter and boil.

(Sauce for same.)

1 table spoon of flour, mixed in cold water; add a cupful of boiling water, stirring as it boils for a minute or two; butter, size of a walnut; 3 tablespoons of sugar, 1 egg; beat all well

together (after melting butter a little, stir rapidly while adding to the flour. Flavoring to taste. Add boiling water if sauce is too thick.

Plum Pudding.
Miss Mary Stover.

1½ cups flour, ½ cup butter, ½ cup molasses, ½ cup sweet milk, ½ teaspoon soda, ½ cup currants, ½ cup raisins. Steam 2 hours and eat with sauce.

Plain Plum Pudding.
J. Dewald.

1 pint of stale bread crumbs, 1 cup flour, 1 cup stoned raisins, juice and rind of 1 lemon, 1 cup of washed currants, 1 cup brown sugar, 1 teaspoon cinnamon, ½ nutmeg, ½ cup molasses, 3 eggs, ½ pound suet, ½ pound citron, ½ teaspoon baking soda: mix well all the dry ingredients. Beat the eggs, add the molasses; dissolve the soda in a tablespoon of hot water. add it to the molasses and eggs, then mix in the dry ingredients and pack into a greased mould; boil 4 hours. Serve with sauce.

Plum Pudding.
Mrs. Chas. Frantz.

½ cup of butter, 2 cups of raisins, chopped; cup sweet milk, 3 cups of flour, cup of molasses, 1 teaspoon of soda, small nutmeg; mix together. Put into a bag and boil 2 hours.

(Sauce for same.)

1 cup of sugar, butter, the size of an egg; 1 egg, 1 tablespoon flour. Mix smooth, then add the grated rind and juice of 2 lemons and a pint of water; let it thicken on the back of stove; do not let it boil.

English Plum Pudding.
Mrs. I. M. Hean.

½ pound suet, 1 pound currants, 1 pound raisins, 1 cup bread crumbs, 2 eggs, ½ pound brown sugar, small quantity of molasses, spices to taste, 1 teaspoon of baking powder. Flour enough to make a very stiff batter; mix with milk or water; boil in muslin bag, 3 hours. Serve with sauce.

Chocolate Pudding.
Mrs. R. H. Graeff.

1 quart of milk, 4 tablespoons of corn starch, 2½ tablespoons

58 .PUDDINGS.

of chocolate, 3 tablespoons sugar; dissolve chocolate in a little boiling water; dissolve corn starch in a little of the milk; heat the remainder of the milk to boiling and stir in the corn starch and sugar, and before it thickens add the chocolate; stir until sufficiently cooked. Use with cream and sugar, or any sauce preferred.

Chocolate Pudding.

Boil 1 quart of milk in which 3 tablespoons of chocolate have been dissolved; stir 3 (scant) tablespoons of corn starch in $\frac{1}{2}$ cup milk, add the yolks of 3 eggs; then pour all in the boiling liquid; stir constantly till it thickens, then add 1 (scant) cup of sugar. Beat the whites of the eggs to a stiff froth, add 5 tablespoons powdered sugar, spread over the top and brown.

Chocolate Custard.
J. Dewald.

Melt 2 ounces of chocolate in a sauce pan, stirring until smooth. Boil a pint of milk, thicken with 4 tablespoons of corn starch. Beat the whites of 4 eggs to a stiff froth, add them with a $\frac{1}{2}$ cup of sugar to the milk. Take from the fire, flavor with vanilla, and to $\frac{1}{2}$ the mixture add the chocolate. Cool the pudding mould, put in the bottom $\frac{1}{2}$ the white mixture. Then all the dark, then the remainder of the white. Set on ice and serve with vanilla cream sauce.

Cream Chocolate Pudding.
Laura Dewald.

1 pint of milk, $1\frac{1}{2}$ cups sugar, 4 eggs, 4 tablespoonfuls corn starch, 2 ounces of chocolate, 1 teaspoonful vanilla. Put the chocolate in a saucepan and stand it over the tea-kettle to melt; stir until perfectly smooth. Put the milk on to boil in a farina boiler. Moisten the corn starch with a little cold water (about $\frac{1}{4}$ cup), and add it to the boiling milk; cook and stir until thick and smooth. Beat the whites of the eggs to a stiff froth; add the sugar to the milk, then the whites, and beat all well together over the fire. Take from the fire, add the vanilla now take out one-third of the mixture; add it to the chocolate; mix well. Dip a plain pudding mould into cold

water; put in the bottom of it half the white mixture, then all the dark, and then all the remainder of the white. Stand on ice for 3 hours to harden. Serve with vanilla sauce poured around it.

Bread Pudding.
Mrs. D. M. Karmany.

Take 2 eggs to 1 pint sweet milk; sugar to sweeten; season with nutmeg; add a little salt. Have slices of stale bread in bottom of pudding pan; then pour over it the custard of milk and eggs. Put in oven hot enough to bake bread. Serve cold or hot. Use wheat bread.

Fairy Pudding.
Mrs. R. H. Graeff.

2 pieces of bread across the loaf, a small piece butter, ½ pint heated milk; pour over the bread and let stand a short time; add ½ cup sugar, 1 egg, ½ cup cut raisins, nutmeg and cinnamon.

Dressing for Same.—Juice of 1 lemon, butter size of walnut, ½ cup sugar, a little nutmeg, 1½ tablespoons water; boil this, then add lemon.

Orange Pudding.
Mrs. J. K. Fisher.

4 large juicy oranges, sweet if possible; 1 pint of sweet milk, 3 eggs, 1 heaping teaspoon corn starch, sugar to taste. Cut the oranges into small pieces, remove seeds, and pour 1 cup of sugar over them; make a custard of the milk and yolks of eggs; when boiling, add corn starch, dissolved in a little of the milk; sweeten to taste. Do not let boil very stiff, and pour it over the oranges. Whip the whites, sweeten to taste, and flavor with vanilla. Place on a buttered plate, and brown in a quick oven. Place the whites on top of pudding. Eat cold. The above is enough for 6 persons.

New Century Pudding.

1 cup of suet, 1 cup of sugar, 1 cup of milk, 2½ cups of flour, 1 cup of raisins, 1 cup of currants, 2 eggs, ½ teaspoonful of salt, 1 teaspoonful of cinnamon, 1 teaspoonful Cleveland baking powder. Chop the suet fine; beat the suet, sugar, and yolks of eggs together till light; then add milk and flour; beat

till smooth; add spices, salt, and whites of eggs; then add the baking powder; mix well, and add fruit, well floured. Turn into a greased mould, and boil for 4 or 5 hours.

Sweet Potato Pudding.
Miss Mary Stover.

1 pint of sweet potatoes, boiled and mashed; 1 cup of sugar, $\frac{1}{2}$ cup of butter, $\frac{1}{2}$ cup of sweet milk, 4 eggs, flavor to taste, 1 tablespoon of baking powder. Bake in a moderate oven 48 minutes. Eat with sauce.

Date Pudding.
R. A. C.

$\frac{1}{2}$ pound of dates, $\frac{1}{4}$ pound grated bread, $2\frac{1}{2}$ ounces sugar, 3 ounces butter, 2 eggs, 1 teacup of milk; chop dates fine. Butter and sprinkle mould with bread crumbs; pour in pudding; cover closely, and boil for 3 hours.

Sweet Potato Pudding.
Mrs. T. Karch.

$\frac{1}{2}$ pound sweet potatoes, juice and rind of 1 lemon, juice and rind of 1 orange, $\frac{1}{4}$ teaspoon of mace, $\frac{1}{4}$ teaspoon of cinnamon, 1 pound sugar, 6 ounces butter, 8 eggs, $\frac{1}{2}$ teaspoon salt.

Cornstarch Pudding.
Mrs. Geo. Stanley.

1 quart of milk, except enough to wet 3 tablespoons of corn starch. Place in a tin pail, set in a kettle of boiling water. Add the yolks of 4 eggs, beaten; $\frac{1}{2}$ cup of sugar, the corn starch, and a little salt. Let it boil until it thickens; flavor with 1 teaspoon of vanilla. Pour into a pudding dish. Beat the whites of the eggs, and pour on top. Place in oven to brown.

Demon Pudding.
Mrs. Crowther.

Melt 6 ounces of butter; pour it over the same quantity of powdered sugar, stirring well till cold. Then grate the rind of a large lemon, and with it 8 eggs, well beaten, and the juice of 2 lemons; stir the whole till it is completely mixed together, and bake the pudding with a paste around the dish.

Suet Pudding.
Mrs. G. W. Jamieson.

1 cup suet, 1 cup milk, 3½ cups flour, 1 tablespoon cloves, cinnamon, a little salt, 1 cup molasses, 1 cup raisins (chopped), 1 egg, 1 nutmeg, 1 teaspoon soda, dissolved in the milk; steam 3 hours. Very nice.

Hard Sauce for Same.—Stir to a cream, 1 cup butter and 3 of powdered sugar; when very light, beat in vanilla or lemon juice.

Peach Pudding.

6 large peaches, 1 pint of flour, 1 egg, ½ teaspoonful of salt, ¾ cup of milk, butter size of an egg, 1 large teaspoon of baking powder. Same can be made using apples.

Huckleberry Pudding.

1 quart of sifted flour; through this rub 1 tablespoon of butter, 3 eggs (beaten separately), 1 dessert spoon baking powder, a pinch of salt, enough sweet milk to make a thick batter, 1 quart of berries, floured. Pour into mould, and steam 3 hours. Serve with sauce.

Judge Peters Pudding.

1 small box of gelatine, dissolved in ½ pint of cold water; then add 1 pint of boiling water, and at the same time 2 cups of sugar and juice of 2 lemons; also 2 bananas, 2 oranges, 6 figs, and 10 English walnuts. Serve with cream. Elegant.

Cocoanut Pudding.
Mrs. R. H. Graeff.

Yolks of 4 eggs, 1 cup sugar, ½ cup bread or sponge cake crumbs, 1 grated cocoanut; also the milk of the nut, if it is not too strong; 1 quart milk, and the whites of 2 eggs, well beaten; grate nutmeg on the top, and bake. Then take the whites of 2 eggs, 2 teaspoons sugar for the icing. Flavor with vanilla, and brown in oven.

Cocoanut Pudding.
Mrs. J. H. Roberts.

1 cocoanut, 1 pint of milk, ½ cup sugar, 1 teaspoonful of vanilla, 3 eggs; beat the eggs all together until light; add the

milk, sugar, vanilla, and cocoanut, grated; stir until thoroughly mixed, and bake in a moderate oven for 30 minutes. Serve cold.

Tapioca Pudding.
Mrs. H. E. Oves.

1 cupful of tapioca; soak it in the evening in a pint of sweet milk; in the morning put it in a pudding pan and boil it till it gets thick; then add 1 egg and the yolks of 2; add sugar enough to taste; then put it in a sauce dish, and beat the whites of 2 eggs to a stiff froth, and put in 2 tablespoonfuls of granulated sugar; then put the froth on the tapioca, and set it in the oven till it browns on top.

Lemon Pudding.
Mrs. John Uhrich.

Grate 1 pound of dry bread; beat together 5 ounces of granulated sugar, 3 ounces of butter, and the yolks of 3 eggs; into this grate the rind of 2 lemons; add the juice of 1 lemon, 1 teaspoon of vanilla. Pour over the crumbs 1 quart of milk, and beat in the other ingredients. Bake ½ hour in a buttered dish. Beat the whites very stiff, with ½ cupful of sugar and a little vanilla. Remove the pudding from the oven; spread the meringue over the top, and return to the oven for 3 minutes.

Lemon Pudding.
Mrs. F. P. Spiese, Tamaqua.

1 pint of bread crumbs, 1 quart of milk, 1 cup of sugar, 4 eggs, 1 lemon, butter the size of an egg. Throw the bread crumbs into the milk; add the sugar, then the beaten yolks of the eggs, the grated rind of the lemon, and the butter, cut into small pieces. Bake in a pudding dish 1 hour, taking care that it does not become watery. Beat the whites of the eggs to a stiff froth; add ½ sugar, and the juice of the lemon. Put jam or jelly on top of the pudding, or not, as preferred. Spread the meringue over it, and set it back in the oven until slightly brown.

Cottage Pudding.
Fannie Atkins.

Sift together 1 pint of flour, a little salt, and 2 heaping teaspoons of baking powder; beat together 3 tablespoonfuls of butter, 1 cup of white sugar; then add 1 egg (beaten), 1 cup of sweet milk, and the flour. Bake in shallow pans. Serve hot, with sauce.

Sauce for Pudding.—Put on the stove 1 pint of water; when it comes to a boil add 2 tablespoonfuls of flour, mixed in cold water; after this boils, pour it over $\frac{1}{2}$ cup of white sugar and 2 tablespoonfuls of butter, that has been worked to a cream.

The pudding and sauce can be flavored with any flavor desired.

Fruit Pudding.
Mrs. Rev. I. C. Fisher.

1 cup sugar, 1 egg, 1 cup sweet cream, 1 heaping cup of flour, $\frac{3}{4}$ teaspoon baking powder. Beat egg and sugar thoroughly; add cream; then flour, and $\frac{1}{2}$ cup of preserved fruit. Bake in cups.

Sauce for Pudding.—1 cup of sugar, 1 cup of water, and butter the size of an egg. Boil together 10 minutes; then pour it on the juice and rind of lemon. If preferred, thicken with corn starch.

Lemon Pudding.
Mrs. Walter Mitchell, Galapolis.

Stir into yolks of 6 eggs one cup sugar, $\frac{1}{2}$ cup water and the grated yellow rind and juice of 2 lemons, soften in warm water 6 crackers or some slices of cake; lay in bottom of a baking dish, pour custard over them; bake till firm; beat whites of eggs to a froth, add 6 tablespoons sugar and beat well. When custard is done, pour frosting over it, return to the oven and brown. Eat either warm or cold.

Prune Pudding.
A Southern Cook.

Wash $\frac{1}{2}$ pound prunes, cover with cold water and let stand over night. In the morning cook till tender, then press through the colander, add $\frac{3}{4}$ cup of granulated sugar and stir till dissolved. Beat the whites of 4 eggs till very stiff, add the prunes carefully and bake 20 minutes in a quick oven. Serve at once, with whipped cream.

Fig Pudding.

Mrs. Edgar Lamoreaux.

Beat 2 eggs, add 1 cup milk, 1 tablespoonful of melted butter, 1 teaspoon of baking powder, 1 cup figs, cut in fine pieces; 1½ cups of flour, turn in a pail greased with butter and steam or boil 2¼ hours or 2 hours.

Sauce for Pudding.—2 ounces butter, beaten to a cream; add 1 cup powdered sugar, slowly beat until it is very light and white, then add 1 egg, beaten very light, and stand in a cold place.

"Punkin Puddin."

A Southern Cook.

To 1 pint of stewed pumpkin add 1 pint of sifted flour, ¼ pound of finely minced suet and 3 eggs, beaten; sweeten to taste with molasses; add allspice to taste, and if not quite the consistency of muffin batter thin it with a little milk. Pour in a pan about inch thick. Bake till brown, and turn together like an omelette.

Lemon Custard.

Miss Mary Stover.

1 lemon, ½ cup butter, 3 cups of sweet milk, 6 eggs, 3 tablespoons of flour, 1 teaspoon of soda; beat the whites of the eggs with 3 tablespoons of sugar, put on the custard when baked brown.

Cream Custard.

Mrs. Ira Rutter.

1 pint new milk, yolks of 2 eggs, ½ cup flour or corn starch, 1 cup sugar; boil and flavor; whites of 2 eggs beaten, with sugar to sweeten. Bake the pie crust first, cover the custard with the meringue, then brown in oven.

Cup Custard.

1 quart milk, 1 cup sugar, 4 eggs, pinch of salt. If liked less sweet, use ¾ cup sugar; beat eggs and pour milk over them; flavor with vanilla, and fill the custard cups; set the cups in a baking pan and half fill with boiling water. Bake in a moderate oven; test with a silver knife; if it comes out smooth and clean they are done.

Tapioca Custard.
Mrs. L.

Soak 1 cup tapioca over night; in the morning put in 1 quart milk; as soon as the milk comes to the boiling point, have ready the yolks of 3 eggs, well beaten in a scant cup of sugar; then stir in and let cook just long enough to thicken or it will whey. Have ready the whites and stir in just as it comes from the fire. Flavor with vanilla.

Lemon Custard.
Mrs. Skinner, York.

2 large lemons, 5 eggs; save 3 whites for icing; 3 tablespoons of flour, 3 cups of sugar, 3 cups of water. Boil until thick; bake the crust and then fill with the icing. Put the whites on top and brown in the oven.

Lemon Custard.
Mrs. C. M. Light.

Yolks of 6 eggs, 6 tablespoons of sugar, 1 grated lemon, 1 pint of sweet milk, 2 tablespoons of melted butter, 2 tablespoons of flour.

Icing.—Whites of 6 eggs, 6 tablespoons of sugar. Bake a little.

Lemon Custard.
Mrs. D. M. Karmany.

1 lemon, 2 cups of sugar, 4 cups sour milk, 3 eggs, 4 tablespoonfuls of flour, 1 teaspoonful of soda, $\frac{1}{4}$ cup butter. Makes 4 pies

Lemon Custard.
Mrs. Irwin H. Bright, Tamaqua.

Line 4 pie pans with pastry; grate 1 large lemon (everything can be grated but the seeds), 2 large cups of sugar, the yolks of 4 eggs; take the whites in a separate bowl and beat to a stiff froth and add, last of all, $\frac{1}{2}$ cup of flour, 2 large cups of water.

Frozen Tapioca Custard.
Abbie Railton.

Soak 6 or 7 ounces of tapioca in 1 quart of milk; when soft, boil 2 quarts of milk, sweetened with $1\frac{1}{4}$ pounds of sugar, then add the tapioca and let it cook 15 minutes. Then stir in 2 ounces of butter and 8 beaten eggs, and take the custard off the fire at once; cool, and flavor with vanilla. Freeze like ice cream. When nearly frozen, add 1 cup of whipped cream and beat well.

Lemon Custard.
Lottie I. Burton, Tamaqua.

1½ cups sugar, 2 large teaspoonfuls of flour, yolks of 3 eggs; beat thoroughly; juice and rind of 2 lemons, 2 cups hot water, butter, size of a walnut; boil until thick. Bake crust and then fill with the custard; cover with meringue made with the whites of 3 eggs and 3 teaspoonfuls of sugar.

Lemon Custard.
Mrs. Walter Randalls, Tamaqua.

Yolks of 3 eggs, ½ cup white sugar, 1 lemon, grated, and squeeze in the juice; 1 tablespoonful of flour, a little salt, 1 cup of sweet milk. Bake same as custard pie, then take whites of 3 eggs, beaten to a froth; 4 tablespoonfuls sugar, a little vanilla; frost the pie and brown in the oven.

Lemon Custard.
Mrs. J. Marshall Funck.

3 boiled potatoes, not so large, mash them up; 2 tablespoonfuls of flour, ¾ pound of sugar, grated rind and piece of lemon, 3 eggs, save whites of 2 for top; 2 pints of water (bake and after done) put whites on top; put a little sugar with whites when you beat them up for top. This will make 2 custards.

Apple Custard.

Pare, cut up and stew 2 pounds of apples; when soft, strain and stir in 1 tablespoonful of butter, ½ pound of sugar, 6 eggs, beaten separately; favor with lemon or vanilla; bake ½ hour. Serve with cream.

Cocoanut Custard.
Mrs. Irwin H. Bright, Tamaqua.

1 cocoanut, butter, the size of a walnut; 1 cup of sugar, 4 eggs, 1 cup of milk; cocoanut is to be added next to last and milk last. Line 4 pie pans with pastry. Bake all together.

Egg Custard.

Emma Kaler Johnson.

1 pint of milk, 2 eggs, 1 tablespoon corn starch. Boil milk.

Chocolate Custard.

Mrs. S. Reinoehl.

1 cup sweet milk, 2 tablespoonfuls grated chocolate, 1 tablespoonful corn starch; heat the above; ¾ cup sugar, yolks of 2 eggs, beaten to a cream; stir together. Flavor with vanilla. Bake well; spread meringue of whites over the top; place again in the oven until brown.

Chocolate Cream Custard.

Mrs. John Knoll.

Scrape ¼ pound of chocolate, pour on it a cupful of boiling water and let stand until it is all dissolved. Beat 8 eggs light, omitting the whites of 2. stir them by degrees into a quart of rich milk alternately with chocolate and 3 tablespoonfuls of white sugar. Put the mixture into cups and bake 10 minutes.

Lemon Custard.

Mrs. Gernet.

1 grated lemon, 3½ cups of milk, 3 tablespoonfuls flour, 1 cup of sugar, 2 tablespoonfuls melted butter, 3 eggs; yolks of eggs, lemon and flour mixed together first; put beaten whites in last.

Orange Custard.

Mrs. J. H. Roberts.

1 grated orange, ½ pound butter, 6 or 8 eggs, a little over a pint of sweet milk.

Potato Custard.

With 5 large potatoes, use 5 eggs, beating the whites light; a ¼ pound of butter, cinnamon or nutmeg to taste. Mash the potatoes very fine. Use milk enough to make a thin batter and sweeten to taste.

Millinery...

YOU will always find the Largest Assortment and Finest Goods at . . . . . .

...Miss L. A. Diehl's,
708 Cumberland Street.

A WOMAN'S EYE FOR BEAUTY
Readily finds the well dressed man in a crowd or on the street. He

CAN WE BE YOUR TAILORS? who is well dressed not only commands the attention of women, but of men alike. . . . . A man is judged somewhat by the fit and make of his clothes. We are proud of the fact that all Clothing made by us . .

Fits Well. Wears Well. Is Low in Price.

I. H. MERKLE & CO.

DESSERTS.

"This same dessert is very pleasant."
"An't please your Honor," quoth the Peasant,
—Pope.

Soft Custard.

1 pint milk, 2 tablespoonfuls sugar, 2 eggs, speck of salt and flavoring. Heat the milk in a double boiler; beat the yolks of the eggs a little, add to them the sugar and salt; pour the heated milk over the mixture and return to the boiler; stir until it thickens; strain, and when cool, flavor. If a thicker custard is desired, use 3 or 4 eggs; the whites beaten to a stiff froth and 2 teaspoonfuls sugar, added, may be served with the custard.

Charlotte Russe.
Mrs. D. M. Sharp.

1 pint milk , 1 pint cream, ½ box gelatine; flavor and sweeten to taste; ¼ pound macaroni; dissolve the gelatine in cold water a few hours. Let the milk come to a boil, pour it on the gelatine, and flavor; strain through a cloth and set in a cool place. Whip the cream light; now line a mould with macaroni; when the milk and gelatine are cold stir in the whipped cream and set away to harden.

Fruit Gelatine.

1 box Cox's gelatine, juice of 3 lemons and 3 oranges, 1½ pounds granulated sugar; put 1 pint cold water on the gelatine; let stand for a couple of hours, then add juice of lemons or oranges, and sugar; after that pour a quart of boiling water, stir well until all is dissolved, then strain and put away to jell partly. Fill a dish with layer of oranges, bananas, white grapes and gelatine and put away to stiffen.

Lemon Jelly.
Mrs. Edgar Lamoreaux, Scranton, Pa.

Box of gelatine in bowl of cold water (1 pint); let stand for 1 hour; pour over that 1½ quarts of boiling water, put in 4 lemons, 2 cups of sugar and set in a cold place to cool.

Gelatine.

2 pints of water on 1 box of Cox's gelatine, 2 pints of water, 2 pounds of sugar, rind and juice of 3 lemons. Put the whole in a kettle, stand on back of stove till all is dissolved and then strain and stand away to cool.

Apple Float.

Roast 8 large apples, core them and fill with sugar, then take 4 eggs, the yolks for dip; thicken with corn starch; the whites thicken with pulverized sugar. Spread over the apples and put in the oven to brown very light. When cold pour over the dip.

Lemon Meringue.
Mrs. P. W. Pratt, Lima, Pa.

1 grated lemon; take 2 cups of hot wataer, mix 2½ tablespoons of corn starch; let boil; when cold, add 2 cups of white sugar, the grated lemon, the yolks of 4 eggs, little nutmeg; then bake. When done, beat the whites to a froth with 6 tablespoonfuls of pulverized sugar, and spread over them; put in the oven and let get a delicate brown. Bake the crusts first.

Lemon Meringue.
Mrs. Jos. Krause.

2 lemons, juice and rind; 2 cups of sugar, 2 cups of water, yolks of 3 eggs, 3 dessert spoonfuls corn starch dissolved in water. Let all come to a boil, so as to thicken, pour on the crusts, which have been previously baked. Beat the whites of the eggs, sweeten, spread on top and bown.

Cream Dessert.

Soak 2 tablespoons of gelatine in not quite ½ cup of warm water; whip 1 pint of rich, sweet cream to the thickness of starch, then strain gelatine in whipped cream, beat 5 minutes longer, then add 7 tablespoons of sugar, add to the cream and beat 10 minutes longer; flavor with vanilla.

German Puffs.
Mrs. Dr. Bruce.

1½ cups of sweet milk, 1½ cups of flour, 2 eggs, beaten; butter, size of an egg. Bake in hot oven.

DESSERTS.

Sicilian Sherbet.
Mrs. Mary H. Parker.

1 quart peaches, cut fine with silver knife; 1 pint orange juice, 1 pound sugar. Freeze very slowly a little over 10 minutes, then as fast as you can for not less than 10 minutes. Pack.

Cream Muffins.
Miss Mary Stover.

1 pint of cream, 2 eggs, 3 cups of sifted flour, 1 teaspoon of salt, 1 tablespoon melted butter, 2 teaspoons of baking powder; beat the yolks of the eggs, add them to the cream, add this gradually to the flour, beat well and let stand 15 minutes, then add the salt, butter, whites of the eggs beaten to a stiff froth; add the baking powder, mix well; bake in gem pans in a quick oven 45 minutes.

Cream Puffs.
Mrs. J. Karch.

Put 2 ounces of butter in a saucepan, with 1½ gills of water; when boiling stir ¼ pound of sifted flour, stir until it thickens; take it off and add 4 eggs, 1 at a time, beating well; drop in buttered puff tins and bake about 20 minutes. Be careful not to take them out of the oven too soon, or they will fall. When done, cut the sides open with a pair of scissors, and put in each 2 tablespoonfuls of the custard, made as follows:

The Custard.—A cup of flour, 1 cup of powdered sugar, 2 eggs and a pint of milk; boil the milk, mix the eggs, flour and sugar together, pour them into the milk, stirring all the time over the fire; flavor with vanilla.

Cream Puffs.

For 1 dozen—½ pint boiling water, and ½ cup of butter; stir in this while boiling, ½ pint flour. Let get cold and add with fork 3 eggs 1 at a time. Drop in a pan and bake 20 minutes.

Cup Puffs.
Miss H. Kendall.

1 pint sweet milk, 1 pint flour, 3 eggs, butter, the size of a walnut; a pinch of salt. Grease cups well. Bake about 20 minutes. Eat with sauce.

Filling for Puffs.

½ pint of new milk, light pinch of salt, 1 tablespoon corn starch, 1 egg, ½ cup sugar; flavor with vanilla.

German Puffs.
Mrs. Karch.

Beat very light the whites of 4 eggs, then beat the yolks and add the whites gradually to them, beating all the time; stir in them 5 tablespoons of flour, and a pinch of salt; add 1 pint of milk; butter teacups, and pour them half full; bake 15 minutes in a hot oven; serve them as soon as baked.

Vanilla Sauce.

1 pint of milk, yolks of 4 eggs, 2 tablespoonfuls of sugar, 1 teaspoonful of vanilla. Put milk in a double boiler to boil; beat the yolks of eggs and sugar together until light, add to the boiling milk, stir over the fire for 2 minutes. Take from fire add vanilla and put on ice to cool.

Blanc Meringue.
Laura Dewald.

1 pint of milk, 3 tablespoonfuls corn starch; boil well; pour in a mould wet with cold water, and serve with vanilla sauce.

1 pint of milk, 2 eggs, beaten separately; 1 teaspoon of vanilla, ½ cup sugar; beat the yolks well, stir in the cold milk, add the sugar and vanilla, and last the whites, beaten well. Have the sauce as cold as possible.

Sallie Lunn.
Laura Dewald.

1 pint of flour, 1 scant teaspoonful of salt, 2 teaspoonfuls of Cleveland baking powder, piece of butter, size of a goose egg; ½ cup sweet milk, 2 eggs; sift flour, baking powder and salt, work in butter, beat eggs and milk together and mix; butter a pie plate and bake ¼ hour.

Floating Island.

1 Make a custard of the yolks of 6 eggs, 1 quart of milk, a small pinch of salt, sugar to taste; place custard in a large tin pan, set on stove, stirring constantly until it boils; flavor, and

DESSERTS. 73

pour into a dish (a shallow, wide one is best); spread smoothly over the boiling-hot custard the well beaten whites. Sprinkle powdered sugar and grated cocoanut on the top.

Baked Pie Plant.
Mrs. Julia A. Strider, Cincinnati.

Cut in pieces about an inch long, put in baking dish in layers with an equal weight of sugar; cover closely and bake.

Apple Dufoy.
Mrs. H. L. Kohler.

Bake 2 tart apples, add to the pulp white of 1 egg, 2-3 cup of sugar; lemon to taste, and beat 30 minutes.

Fruit Gelatine.
Julia Lord.

1 box of gelatine, soaked in 1 pint of cold water; add 1 quart of boiling water, juice of 6 lemons, 2 pounds sugar, 4 oranges, torn into small shreds; 4 bananas, sliced; ½ pound white grapes, seeded; arrange fruit in layers and pour the gelatine over.

Gelatine.
Mrs. J. K. Fisher.

½ box gelatine, pour over it 1 cup of cold water, soak a few hours; add 1 pint of boiling water, 1 cup of sugar, juice of 1 lemon; strain all.

Tapioca Cream.
Mrs. B. F. Knerr, Chicago.

Soak over night ½ cup tapioca; in the morning put on to boil 1 quart of milk (use double boiler to avoid scorching), beat light the yolks of 2 eggs and stir in the milk, add the tapioca and 5 tablespoonfuls sugar; boil 20 minutes; add 1 tablespoonful vanilla; allow to cool; beat light the whites of 2 eggs, add teaspoonful vanilla in this, 2 tablespoonfuls pulverized sugar; stir this into sauce very lightly. Put on ice.

Brown Betty.
Laura Dewald.

Pare, core and slice 6 or 7 tart apples; put a layer of stale bread crumbs in the bottom of a baking dish, then a layer of the apples, then another layer of bread crumbs, and another layer of apples, and so on until all is used, having the last layer crumbs; add ½ cup water to ½ cup molasses, stir in 2 tablespoonfuls of brown sugar; pour it over the crumbs and bake in a moderate oven for 1 hour. Serve hot with sweetened cream or hard sauce.

Delicious Dessert.
Miss Alice Scott.

Take a sufficient number of bananas, slice thin, put in a dish in layers; over each layer sprinkle sugar and pouring juice of lemon over.

A Fancy Dessert.

Place layer of sliced oranges on bottom of a glass dish, cover with powdered sugar and then a thick layer of cocoanut; repeat this until dish is full.

A Simple Dessert.
Mrs. Henry Houck.

Line the sides of a pudding dish with sponge cake and the bottom with sliced bananas; fill the dish with whipped cream; set on ice until wanted.

Orange Float.
Mrs. R. H. Graeff.

Mix 1 quart of water, the juice and pulp of 2 lemons, 1 cup of sugar. Boil sufficiently to dissolve the sugar, then strain and again bring to a boil, and add 4 tablespoonfuls of corn starch, mixed in a little cold water; stir and boil 15 minutes; when cool, pour it over 4 or 5 sliced oranges; over top spread the beaten whites of 3 eggs sweetened, and a few drops of vanilla. Eaten with cream.

Strawberry Shortcake.
Amelia Ohlwiler, Altoona, Pa.

2 heaping teaspoons Cleveland baking powder sifted with 1 quart flour, ½ teacup butter, 1 tablespoon sugar, a little salt, enough sweet milk or water to make a soft dough; roll out almost as thin as pie crust; place a layer in a baking pan and spread with very little butter upon which sprinkle a little flour,

DESSERTS.

then add another layer of crust as before until the crust is all used, or bake in 2 baking tins—this makes 4 layers. Bake 15 minutes in a quick oven, separate when done, put plenty of sweetened strawberries between; serve with sugar and cream or whipped cream.

Strawberry Shortcake.

1 quart flour, 1 cup butter, 3 teaspoons Cleveland baking powder, $\frac{1}{2}$ salt spoon of salt, the white of 1 egg; rub the butter into the flour, then add the baking powder and salt. Beat the white of the egg to a stiff froth and add with cold milk sufficient to make a dough stiff enough to roll out. Make the cakes about $\frac{1}{2}$ inch thick and bake in pie tins in a quick oven. When done cut around the edges and split them, place a layer of well sugared berries between, sift powdered sugar over the top and serve with cream.

Floating Island.
Anna M. Hammer.

Whites of 6 eggs—more or less as required,—this quantity would answer for a family of 6 or 8; add 1 tablespoon of currant jelly (raspberry jelly added is fine—3 of each) to each egg and 1 tablespoon of sugar to each egg; beat all together till able to turn upside down. Float on milk and eat with crackers and cream.

Apple Tapioca.
Mrs. Geo. Stanley.

Soak 1 cup tapioca in 3 pints cold water over night; boil 20 or 30 minutes; add $1\frac{1}{2}$ quarts of pared and quartered apples, 1 cup sugar, 1 teaspoon salt, essence of lemon; put into buttered dish; bake $1\frac{1}{4}$ hours. Serve with cream and sugar.

Orange Meringue.

Cut 6 oranges fine, taking out the seeds; add 1 cup of sugar; beat the yolks of 3 eggs, 1 pint of milk, $1\frac{1}{2}$ cups of sugar, $1\frac{1}{2}$ tablespoons of corn starch; boil; when thick turn over the oranges; the whites of the eggs and $\frac{1}{2}$ cup of sugar beaten light and put on top when cold.

Strawberry Shortcake.

1 quart flour, 2 teaspoons Cleveland baking powder, ½ cup butter and lard mixed, ½ pint milk, 3 tablespoons sugar.

Charlotte Russe.
Mrs. D. M. Karmany.

1 pint (thick) sweet cream, whites of 4 eggs, 1 cup pulverized sugar; flavor with vanilla; beat the eggs to a stiff froth, add cream and beat again until well thickened, then add sugar and flavor. Pour over slices of sponge cake.

Charlotte Russe.

1 quart sweet cream, 1 pint sweet milk, ½ box Cox's gelatine, ½ pound macaroons, dissolve the gelatine in water, let the milk come to a boil, add about a cup of sugar to the milk, then the gelatine; strain this and put out to cool; when cool, flavor with vanilla, add the cream, well whipped; beat this again, lay the macaroons in the bottom of your pudding dish and pour the pudding over them.

Charlotte Russe.
Mrs. E. C. Hoffer.

Soak ¼ box of gelatine about ½ hour in ¾ cup of cold water, then set in a bowl of boiling water to dissolve; whip 1 quart cream until stiff, sweeten with a goblet of sugar, pour on the gelatine and beat all together. Flavor to taste.

Orange Sherbet.
Mrs. John T. Atkins.

1 pint of orange juice, 2 tablespoonfuls of gelatine, 1 pound of sugar, 1 quart of water; cover the gelatine with a little cold water and soak ½ hour; boil the sugar and water together for 5 minutes, add the gelatine and stand away to cool; when cold add the orange juice and strain through a fine sieve; freeze and add the meringue.

Meringue.—Beat the white of 1 egg frothy, then add a tablespoon of pulverized sugar and beat stiff; remove the dasher and stir in the meringue. Repack, and stand away ready for use.

ICES AND CREAMS.

Cheese Souffle.

2 tablespoonfuls butter, 1 heaping tablespoonful flour, ½ cup milk, 1 cup grated cheese, 3 eggs, ½ tablespoonful salt, spark cayenne. Put the butter in a saucepan, and, when hot, add the flour, and stir until smooth; add the milk and seasoning; cook 2 minutes and then add the well beaten yolks of the eggs and the cheese. Set away to cool; when cold add the whites of the eggs beaten to a stiff froth. Turn into a buttered dish and bake 20 to 25 minutes. Serve the moment it comes from the oven.

Orange Souffle.

Peel and slice 6 oranges, put in a glass dish a layer of oranges, then 1 of sugar, and so on until all the orange is used; let stand 2 hours; make a soft-boiled custard of yolks of 3 eggs, pint of milk, sugar to taste, with grating of orange peel for flavor, and pour over the oranges when cool enough not to break dish; beat whites of the eggs to a stiff froth, stir in sugar, and put over the pudding.

Cream Chocolate Pudding.
Miss Alice Scott.

1 pint of milk, ½ cup sugar, 4 eggs, 4 tablespoonfuls corn starch, 2 ounces chocolate, 1 teaspoonful vanilla. Put the chocolate in a sauce pan to melt over the tea-kettle, stir until perfectly smooth; put the milk on to boil in a double boiler, moisten the corn starch with a little cold water (about ¼ cup), add it to the boiling milk, cook and stir till thick and smooth; beat the whites of eggs to a stiff froth, add the sugar to the milk, then the whites of the eggs; beat all well together, over the fire; take from the fire, add the vanilla, take out one-third of the mixture, add to it the chocolate; mix well. Dip a plain pudding mould in cold water, put in the bottom of it ½ the white, then all the dark, the remainder of white; put on ice to cool. Serve with vanilla sauce.

Sando's

DRY GOODS AND NOTION HOUSE.

...THE PLACE TO GET YOUR...

ONE PRICE STORE

DRESS GOODS, FANCY GOODS, RIBBONS, LACES, VEILINGS, KID GLOVES, HANDKERCHIEFS, CORSETS, TABLE LINENS, NAPKINS, TOWELS, ETC., at Low Prices.

Peter Sando, 757 and 759 Cumberland St. ...LEBANON, PA...

The Proof of the Pudding
is in the Eating.

So with our Spices, Flavoring Extracts, Cooking and Baking Necessaries. We do not claim to be the Cheapest, but do claim to handle nothing but the Finest and Best regardless of price . . . .

Chas. H. Blouch, Druggist,
521 Cumberland Street,   Lebanon, Pa.

Wild Cherry Lung Balsam

For Coughs, Colds, Asthma, and all Throat and Lung Troubles. Absolutely guaranteed to do what we claim for it or will refund the money.

ICES AND CREAMS.

Velvet Cream.
Miss Ella Houseman.

1 pint of the very best cream, 1 heaping tablespoon of gelatine; put gelatine in a cup with a little water to dissolve it; sugar to suit the taste; whip the cream, add the sugar and afterward the gelatine. Flavor to taste.

Frozen Bananas.
Mrs K. H. Mish.

Cut 6 large, ripe, red bananas crosswise in thin slices; add ½ pound of powdered sugar to them; let stand 1 hour; then add a quart of water and grated peel of a lemon. When the sugar is dissolved put the fruit in, and freeze as you would ice cream.

Velvet Cream.
Mrs. H. T. Atkins.

1 quart of good cream, ¾ cup of powdered sugar, 1 tablespoon of vanilla, ½ box gelatine. Cover the gelatine with ½ cup of cold water and soak ½ hour. Add to the soaked gelatine just enough boiling water to dissolve it. Then add the sugar and cream, then the vanilla. Put it in moulds to harden. It is best made the day before using, unless put on ice to harden.

Velvet Cream.
Mrs. T. Karch.

1 pint of cream, 2 tablespoons of Cox's gelatine, dissolved in a little cream; 2 tablespoons of sugar, 1 tablespoon of vanilla. Put on ice.

Frozen Strawberries.

1 quart berries, juice of 2 lemons, 1 pound sugar, 1 quart water; add sugar and lemon juice to berries; let stand 1 hour. Mash the berries, add water and stir until sugar is dissolved; freeze same as ice cream.

Orange Water Ice.
Mrs. Emma P. Grittinger.

12 large oranges, if small 14; juice of 1 lemon, or 2 if desired. Put on the stove 3 pints of water to 1 good pint of sugar and chip the rind of 2 oranges and put to the water and sugar; when heated put away to get cold. When cold, take out the rind and add the juice of the oranges; strain, and it is then ready for freezing. Whip about 1 good pint of cream and when serving put on each plate 1 spoonful.

Lemon Water Ice.
Mrs. D. M. Karmany.

6 lemons, 1 quart water, 1 pint cream, grated rind of 2 of the lemons, 1 pound powdered sugar; add together and strain. Freeze as ice cream.

Frozen Custard.
Miss Bertha Ramsay.

1 quart milk, 3 eggs, 1 tablespoon corn starch; sweeten to taste. Let come to a boil, stirring all the time; flavor.

Lemon Water Ice.
Fannie Atkins.

4 large, juicy lemons, 1 quart of water, 1 orange, 1¼ pounds of sugar. Put the sugar and water on to boil, chip the yellow rind from 3 lemons and the orange, add to the syrup; boil 5 minutes and stand away to cool. Squeeze the juice from the orange and the 4 lemons, add it to the cold syrup, and strain through a cloth; freeze the same as ice cream. Water ice need not be turned all the time.

Ice Cream.
Mrs. R. Hean.

1 quart milk, 5 eggs, yolks and whites beaten separately; 3½ cups sugar, 3 pints rich cream, 4 teaspoons vanilla or other flavor. Heat the milk almost to boiling, stir in gradually the beaten yolks and sugar, beating constantly; add the whites and return to the fire, boiling in a pan set within another of hot water; boil 15 minutes; when quite cold, beat in the cream and flavoring. Will make 5 or 6 quarts of cream.

[handwritten at top: 1 pt water, 1/2 lb sugar, 1/2 pt milk, grated rind of]

ICES AND CREAMS.

Frozen Custard.
Emma Richards.

1 quart milk, 4 eggs, 1½ small cups of sugar, separate the whites from the yolks, beat the latter with the sugar; add the milk and strain; then boil in a double boiler. When perfectly cold, add the well beaten whites, with flavoring to taste, and freeze.

Baked Pears.
Mrs. I M. Hean.

Stand the pears in an earthen dish, pour around them a cup of boiling water; add 4 tablespoonfuls of sugar; cover and bake slowly until pears are tender, basting 3 or 4 times; when cool, serve with sugar and cream.

Banana Cream.

After peeling the bananas mash them with an iron or wooden spoon; allow equal quantities of bananas and sweet cream to 1 quart of mixture; allow ¼ pound sugar. Beat them all together until the cream is light.

Banana Cream.

Boil a pint of milk in which has been dissolved a cupful of sugar; stir a heaping tablespoonful of corn starch in a cup of cold milk, add a beaten egg; pour all into the boiling liquid, When all have come to a boil, pour half the mixture in a glass pudding dish; let cool on the ice; slice 2 large bananas on top, then pour on the rest of the custard. When firm add another layer of sliced bananas.

Ice Cream.
Mrs. Ira Rutter.

1½ quarts cream, 1 pint milk, 3 eggs, 1 pound sugar; boil sugar, milk and the yolk of egg in a double boiler; when cold add the cream, then put in the freezer and when it begins to freeze add the whites beaten light; flavor to taste.

Water Ice.

To a quart of water add 1 pound of sugar, flavor to taste and freeze.

Frozen Custard.
Mrs. J. H. Roberts.

3 pints new milk, 1 pint cream, 3 eggs; bring the milk almost to a boil, and pour carefully over the eggs after they are well beaten; add to this 1 pound sugar and flavoring to taste. When cool, add the cream, and it is ready to freeze.

Cream for Filling.

½ cup sugar, 1 cup milk, 3 heaping teaspoons corn starch. Fill the puffs just before tea. Flavor with vanilla.

Ice Cream.

3 quarts of cream, 1 quart of milk, 1 small teaspoon of corn starch, 1 vanilla bean, yolk of one egg; put the milk, egg, and corn starch on to boil, cutting the bean into fine pieces; 1½ pounds of sugar. Strain and add cream and freeze.

Chocolate Ice Cream.

Put a quart of cream in saucepan with 4 ounces of grated chocolate, ½ pound of sugar, a tablespoonful of extract of vanilla, and a pinch of powdered cinnamon. Put on the stove and stir until it boils; strain, add a pint of cold cream. When cold, pour in the freezer and freeze.

Snow Balls.
E. D. M.

2 cups milk, 2 tablespoons corn starch, mixed in a little water; ½ cup sugar; boil 5 minutes, flavor, add whites of 3 eggs.

Sauce.—Boil 1 pint of milk and yellows of 3 eggs; sweeten and flavor.

American Cream.
Miss Ella Hauer.

½ box gelatine, 1 cup sugar, 4 eggs, 1 quart sweet milk; soak gelatine ½ hour in 1 pint of milk; beat yolks of eggs and sugar, then add rest of milk; when at boiling point add dissolved gelatine. Let it boil thoroughly, stirring constantly, then pour into the whites of eggs beaten to a stiff froth. Stir well and put into mould.

ICES AND CREAMS.

Spanish Cream.
Miss Mary Stover.

1 quart of milk, 1-3 box gelatine; let it come to a boil; beat the yolks of 4 eggs with little milk, add 7 tablespoons of sugar and the yolks of the eggs; boil until thick; flavor with vanilla: beat the whites of the eggs to a froth, mix, set on ice to cool, and stir a few times till it gets thick.

Chocolate Cream.
Mrs. J. W.

1 cup grated chocolate, sufficient cold water to wet it; beat the yolks of 5 eggs, $\frac{1}{2}$ cup sweet cream, $\frac{1}{2}$ cup sugar; stir in the chocolate; let it boil until it thickens; when cold ice the cake.

Boston Cream Puffs.
Mrs. Chas. Rockel, Allentown, Pa.

1 cup hot water, $\frac{1}{2}$ cup butter; put into a vessel on the stove; while boiling add 1 cup flour, stirring constantly; when this is cold, add 3 eggs (not beaten), and bake in 15 puffs.

Ice Cream.
E. Richards.

1 quart and pint of cream, $1\frac{1}{2}$ pints of milk, 2 eggs; beat the eggs and 1 cup of sugar together; then add your milk, and dissolve a teaspoon of corn starch in milk; boil in double boiler; when cold add cream, then flavor and freeze.

Vanilla Ice Cream.
Mrs. J. E. M.

2 quarts milk, 2 quarts cream, 1 cup flour, 2 pound sugar, 4 eggs, 4 teaspoons vanilla; boil the milk, flour and yolks of eggs and sugar, then strain; beat whites of eggs to froth and with cream after partly frozen; let get perfectly cold before straining, after boiling.

Spanish Cream.
Mrs. M. A. McFarland.

1 ounce of isinglass, 3 pints of milk, 6 eggs, 8 tablespoons of sugar; soak gelatine 1 hour in milk, then let come to a boil; beat the yolks with sugar, add to; beat the whites and put on top.

Banks Bros.

G. W. Jamieson, Manager. Department Store

...727 Cumberland Street,

LEBANON, PA.

The Mecca for... Young People Just Going to Housekeeping....

Full line of Dinner and Toilet Sets, Pictures, Table and Floor Oil-Cloths, Tubs, Wash Baskets, Tinware, Graniteware, Glassware, Toys, School Supplies, Hosiery and Notions. . . . .

We make a specialty in giving the greatest values for the least money—a living profit and honest dealing, our motto.

We make a specialty of Grindley's W. H. English Ironstone China, in sets or open stock, and guarantee every piece.

Look for...

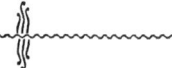 White Front.

Dont... ✸
Mistake
✸ The Place.

PIES.

*"No soil upon earth is so dear to our eyes,
As the soil we first stirred in terrestrial pies."*
—O. W. Holmes.

Cream Strawberry Tart.

Put your strawberries in layers in a deep puff paste crust, sprinkling each layer thickly with sugar. Put on a very thick top crust with a broad slit in it. Bake the pie, and when done pour through this slit the following mixture:

Heat to boiling ½ cup of milk and ½ cup of cream; while boiling add the whites of 2 eggs beaten light, a tablespoonful of sifted sugar, and a small teaspoonful of corn starch made into a paste with cold milk. Beat these 3 minutes, stirring until quite smooth. Let get nearly cold before pouring into the crust. Serve cold.

Jenny Lynn Pie.
Mrs. I M. Hean.

1 cup bread crumbs, 1 cup sugar, ½ cup molasses, 1 cup water, a little more than ½ a cup of vinegar, 1 egg, 1 teaspoonful of cinnamon, cloves, allspice and soda; scald soda and put in last.

Lemon Tart.

Grate 1 lemon, 2 cups sugar, 2½ cups water, ½ cup flour, 4 eggs, butter, the size of a walnut; make a rich pie crust to line the pans. This makes 2 tarts.

Lemon Tart.
Mrs. H. V. Greiner.

1 lemon, 2 teaspoonfuls butter, 2 tablespoonfuls flour, 2 cups sweet milk, 2 cups sugar, 2 eggs.

Lemon Pie.

1 grated lemon, 1 cup of sugar, 2 tablespoonfuls of corn starch, 1 egg, 1 cup of water; boil water and add corn starch and sugar; when cool put lemon and beaten egg in butter size of an egg. Bake between crusts like pie. Boil it just like corn starch, and when cool put in your pies.

Lemon Pie.

1 egg, 2 teacupfuls of white sugar, 2 teacupfuls of boiling water, 1 tablespoon of butter, 2 small spoons of corn starch, 2 lemons. Dissolve the corn starch in a little cold water, add the sugar to boiling water, let it boil a few minutes, set aside to cool, then add the butter, egg and lemons.

Lemon Pie.
Elma Fry, Pleasant Grove.

½ cup butter, ½ cup flour, ½ cup water, 2 cups sugar, 1 lemon, 3 eggs.

Lemon Pie.

2 lemons, 3 cups sugar, 5 cups water, 4 tablespoonfuls of corn starch, 4 eggs. (Elegant.)

Water Lemon Pie.
Mrs. C. A. Bell.

Line 2 tin pie dishes with paste and bake; boil in a pan 2 cups sugar, 1 grated lemon, 2 cups cold water, 4 minutes; 2 tablespoons corn starch, 2 yolks of eggs, keep the whites out and after the boiled custard is put in the baked crust, beat the whites stiff and add 1 tablespoonful sugar, spread on top and brown 1 minute. These are good, cheap and easy to make.

Lemon Pie.
Mrs. W. E. Scobey.

1 lemon, grated; 1 cup sugar, the yolks of 3 eggs, small piece butter, 3 tablespoons milk, 1 teaspoon corn starch; beat all together and bake in a rich crust. Beat the whites with 3 tablespoons sugar, place on the pie when done and then brown in the oven.

Pie Crust.

2 quarts of flour, 1 teaspoon salt, 4 teaspoons Cleveland baking powder. Sieve all together; 2 coffee cups of lard and mix thoroughly. This quantity will last a month. Can be mixed and set away ready to use at any time. When ready to make a pie, take a coffee cup of this mixture, wet with a little cold water in a pan, mix with a knife, put on a board and roll out without kneading.

Cottolene requires only 2-3 the quantity of lard. Use it.

Pie Crust.

1 cup of flour, butter size of an egg, pinch of salt, 1 scant teaspoon Cleveland baking powder. Wet with cold milk.

Orange Pie.

1 cup sugar, 2 tablespoons flour mixed with sugar; then add juice and rind of 1 orange, 1 egg, with yolks of 2 more, saving whites for frosting. Enough milk to fill a rather deep pie plate half full after it is lined with crust. Bake long enough to brown and set the custard. Beat thoroughly the whites of the 2 eggs to a stiff froth, add 2 tablespoons white sugar, cover pie, and bake to a light brown.

Custard Pie.

4 eggs, 1 quart milk, ½ cup sugar, salt and nutmeg to taste. Beat eggs and sugar together, and add to the heated milk. Will make 2 pies.

Chocolate Pie.

Make 1 crust and bake a little. Then take 2 cups milk, and let it come to a boil, 3 tablespoons chocolate, 1 tablespoon corn starch, 3 tablespoons sugar, 3 eggs, yolks. Stir into the milk until it thickens. Pour into crust and bake a few minutes. Beat the whites of 3 eggs, add sugar, spread on top and brown.

Potato Pie.

Take about a pint of cold mashed potatoes. Add ½ cup of butter, 2 eggs, ½ a lemon, a little nutmeg, and a little cream or milk to thin it. Sweten to taste with about 1 cup of sugar. Will make 2 small pies.

Raisin Pie.

½ a pound of raisins stewed with a few grapes, cherries, currants, or any kind of berries, will make 2 pies baked in a shallow tin, with a delicate upper crust. Dredge the fruit with flour if there is too much juice.

Berry Pies.

Berry pies should be well dredged with flour before putting on the upper crust. Sweeten according to the tartness of the fruit. No water is needed.

Cottolene requires only 2-3 the quantity of lard. Use it.

PIES.

Dried Apple Pie.

2-3 of a cup of mashed apples, 1 cup sweet cream, 1 egg. Sugar to taste.

Dried Peach Pie.

An excellent pie can be made of dried peaches. Let the peaches soak in cold water over night. Stew them in the same water until so soft that you can mash them fine.

For One Pie.—Add 2 tablespoonfuls sweet cream and a little more, $\frac{1}{2}$ cup of sugar (too much sugar destroys the flavor of the fruit. Butter may be used in place of the cream, but if possible use the cream, as it gives such smoothness to the filling.

Apple Tart Pie.

Line a pie tin with a crust. Pare apples, cut in two crossways, take out core, place in pan with 1 cup sugar, cinnamon, and pieces of butter. Sift a tablespoonful of flour over. Add 1 cup of water.

Currant Pie.

Line a deep tin with puff paste. For 1 pie use 1 cup ripe currants and 1 cup sugar. Jam these together thoroughly, and add 1 tablespoonful of flour. Use top crust and bake quickly.

Apple Dumplings.

Mrs. G. W. Gaverich.

4 cups of flour, a spoonful of Cleveland baking powder to each cup of flour, a lump of butter about the size of a shelled walnut; milk enough to make a soft dough; a pinch of salt.

Apple Pie.

Fill the pie crust with juicy apples sliced very thin. Put on an upper crust and bake until the apples are soft. Then remove upper crust and add sugar, butter and grated nutmeg or cinnamon. Stir through the apple and replace the crust.

Shoefly Pie.

4 cups of flour, $\frac{3}{4}$ cup of butter, 1 cup of sugar; mix these together for the crumbs; take dish, put in 1 cup of molasses, 1 cup boiling water, 1 teaspoonful of soda; cover 4 pans with pie crust; put in thin mixture, then the crumbs, then bake.

Cottolene requires only 2-3 the quantity of lard. Use it.

Perfect Pie.

2 eggs, 2 tablespoonfuls corn starch, 5 tablespoonfuls sugar, 1 quart of milk. Bake in one crust; when it begins to bake sprinkle a small cupful of cocoanut over the top and it will fall through the custard. Make a frosting for the top if desired.

Mince Meat.
Mrs. Rev. A. M. Stirk, Allentown

5 pounds of apples, 4 pounds of beef, 2 pounds of raisins, 2 pounds of currants, 1 pound of citron, 2 oranges, 2 lemons, 2 nutmegs; other spices to suit the taste. Mix with sweet cider.

Mince Meat.
Mrs. Hockley.

6 pounds of lean beef, well cooked; 2 pounds of suet, ¼ peck of highly flavored apples, 1 pound of citron; chop these fine, 1½ pounds of seedless raisins, 2 pounds of currants, ½ peel of orange. cut fine; make it sharp with salt, sugar, cinnamon and nutmeg. Set away in a cool place for a week or 10 days, then it is ready for use. Thin out with sweet cider.

[Note.] Cider can be kept sweet by taking from the press, boiling and bottling air-tight until used.

Cocoanut Tart.
Mrs. Ira Rutter.

2 eggs or whites of 4, 1 cup of sweet milk, 2 cups of sugar, 1 grated cocoanut, butter, the size of an egg, 3 tablespoons of cracker dust.

Cocoanut Pie.
Mrs. D. M. Karmany.

6 eggs, ½ cup butter, 2 cups sugar, 2 tablespoonfuls flour, 1 quart sweet milk, 1 large cocoanut, grated; beat all together. This makes 4 pies.

Cream Pie.
Mrs. D. M. Karmany.

1 pint sweet cream, (good and rich) sweetened and flavored to taste; beat light with egg beater. Have crusts for 2 pies previously baked of nice puff paste When cold put on the cream.

Cottolene requires only 2-3 the quantity of lard. Use it.

Cream Pie.

Bake your shell before putting in filling. Filling—1 quart of milk, 3 eggs, ½ cup of flour, ½ cup of sugar; mix the yolks of the eggs, flour and sugar in a little milk; put the remaining milk on to boil, then add the mixture, stirring all the time. Boil a few minutes then flavor. Beat the whites of eggs with a little sugar; when done spread on top.

Cream Pie.

Beat the yolks of 3 eggs with ½ cup sugar and little nutmeg, cinnamon or lemon; add a tablespoon of soft butter and beat again; stir in a cup of sweet cream, a little salt; pour the mixture into the crust and bake at once. Beat the whites of eggs stiffly with a heaping tablespoon of sugar and juice of ¼ lemon, spread over the pie and return to the oven for a moment to lightly brown.

Sugar Pie.
Mrs. Mary Ashmead.

1 pound sugar, ¾ cup butter and lard, 3 eggs, 2 teaspoonfuls of Cleveland baking powder, 1½ cups of sweet milk, 4 cups of flour

Pumpkin Pie.

1 pint pumpkins, 1 pound sugar, ½ pound butter, beaten to a cream; 5 eggs, 1 quart sweet milk, 2 tablespoons flour, little cinnamon; beat the whites to a froth and stir in last. Good.

Apple Dumplings.
Mrs. Richards, Tamaqua.

Whites of 3 eggs, beaten to a stiff froth; 1 coffee cup of rich cream, level teaspoon of best soda; add flour to form a smooth dough; knead well, and put in a warm place for 2 hours. Lay 2 quarters together, wrap a bit of dough spread out with the hands well around them, fasten the edges well, roll in flour, and drop in kettle of briskly boiling water, and keep boiling for 15 minutes; eat with sweetened cream. This will make 8 good dumplings.

Banana Pie.

Slice raw bananas. Add butter, sugar, allspice and vinegar (or boiled cider, or diluted jelly). Bake with two crusts.

Cottolene requires only 2-3 the quantity of lard. Use it.

BREAD.

Bread made by the two following recipes is much more healthful than yeast bread, and is especially recommended to those of weak digestion. Because of its wholesomeness we call it Peptik Bread.

It is made without yeast, does not contain any yeast germs, and will not ferment in the stomach. It will never be sour and contains all the nutrient properties of the flour.

Besides, it is easily made. It can be made ready for the oven in five minutes without the hands touching the dough.

Many physicians are recommending the Peptik Graham Bread to their patients who suffer from indigestion.

Good bread makes a poor meal acceptable, while the most luxurious table is spoiled without it. Light crisp rolls for breakfast; good, sweet bread for dinner, and flaky biscuit for supper, truly prepare a man to rise early in the morning (good naturedly) to prove the old adage,

"Makes a man healthy, wealthy and wise."

In making bread everything depends upon three things: good flour, good yeast, and strength to knead it well. One cannot make good bread out of poor materials. A good rule to guide one in kneading, is to knead until it does not stick to the board. The oven should be kept at a moderate heat, (and not allowed to cool and then heat up again), but rather get cooler as the bread is baking. When bread is taken from the oven it should always be wrapped up well in a cloth.

Peptik Graham Bread.

For one loaf.—3 cups Graham flour, 1 cup white flour, $1\frac{1}{2}$ teaspoonfuls salt, $2\frac{1}{2}$ teaspoonfuls Cleveland's Baking Powder. Put these ingredients in a bowl, mix well with a spoon. Make a well in center, pour in 1 large tablespoonful Orleans molasses and 1 pint of water. With a large spoon stir quickly and thoroughly together. When all the flour is wet stir it a moment longer, then turn at once into a well greased baking pan 4 inches wide, 4 inches deep, and 8 inches long. Smooth the top of the dough with a knife dipped in melted butter. Bake at once, in a moderate oven, $1\frac{1}{4}$ hours. As soon as baked remove from the pan, sprinkle with water and wrap in bread cloth until cold.

Hop and Potato Yeast.

Pare 10 medium size potatoes; put 2 quarts of water in a porcelain kettel, into which put a large handful of hops, put into a thin cloth bag tied close. Set the whole on the fire and let it boil until the potatoes are done. Put a large handful of flour in a crock. Pour the liquid on the flour and stir briskly, leaving the potatoes in the kettle. Mash them smooth free from lumps. When this is done turn them in the crock, and beat the whole thoroughly. If the batter is too stiff add a little boiling water, squeezing the hop bag in the water. Set in a cool place, and when cool stir in a small teacup of yeast, or a cake of compressed yeast. Put in a warm place to rise. When it commences to rise stir down several times briskly. When raised sufficiently, stir in a tablespoonful of salt and the same of sugar, and let it stand in the kitchen until it falls. Then set in a cool place and tie up tightly. This yeast will keep a month.

Making Bread.

In the evening take 5 or 6 little potatoes for each loaf ot bread. Wash them clean and boil with their jackets on; when done mash them with their jackets on and add as much water as necessary for the number of loaves of bread you wish to make. When cool enough add yeast, a little salt and 1 cup of flour, stir well, keep warm and set to rise over night. In the morning strain through a colander and add enough flour to make a stiff batter and beat until smooth. The rising will be light as foam.

Potato Yeast.

12 good sized potatoes, 1 cup brown sugar, 1 cup flour, 1 cup salt, 1 tablespoonful ginger. Put a handful of hops in a bag and boil with potatoes in 2 quarts of water. Take this water and scald the flour, etc. When cool add 2 yeast cakes. Set to rise in a warm place for 20 hours. Bottle for use.

Dry Yeast.

Boil 2 large potatoes and a handful of hops (the latter in a bag) in 3 pints of water. When done take out the potatoes, mash well; add 1 pint of flour and pour boiling water over all.

Cottolene requires only 2-3 the quantity of lard. Use it.

Beat well together, adding 1 tablespoon of salt, 1 of ginger and ½ cup sugar. When lukewarm add 1 cup of good yeast and let it stand 2 days (or if very warm weather only 1 day) stirring down frequently. Add good white cornmeal until thick enough to make into cakes about ½ inch in thickness. Place to dry in the shade (never expose to sun or hot stove) where the air will pass freely so as dry them as soon as possible, for fermentation goes on as long as there is any moisture. Turn the cakes frequently, breaking them up somewhat, or even crumbling them so they will dry out evenly. When thoroughly dried put in a paper sack and keep in a dry place. A small cake will make a sponge sufficient to bake 5 or 6 ordinary loaves.

Salt Rising Bread.

For Yeast.—Scald ½ cup new milk; when cool thicken with cornmeal about like pancake batter. Keep warm 4 or 5 hours. It should then be light. Stir often first 2 hours.

For Bread.—Sift enough flour for 3 loaves and a little more, so as to have some the same temperature to knead it out with. Make a hole in the center of the flour. Take 1 pint of good sweet milk and add 1 quart boiling water; pour slowly in center of flour,stirring it gradually until you have a stiff batter, then stir in yeast. Put a litle flour over the top. Set over warm water until light—it takes about an hour and a half. When light it is ready for loaves. Knead well but not hard. Set each loaf over a saucer of warm water and keep in a warm place about an hour, or until light, and then bake.

Whole Wheat Bread.
Mrs. John Urich.

1 pint of milk, heated to boiling point; allow to cool; ½ yeast cake; set the sponge with milk and yeast to rise 3 hours in a warm place. Work into pans and bake 1 hour.

French Crackers.

6 eggs, 12 tablespoonfuls of sweet milk, 6 tablespoonfuls of butter, ¼ teaspoonful of soda; mould with flour, pounding and working ½ an hour; roll it thin; bake with rather quick fire.

Cottolene requires only 2-3 the quantity of lard. Use it.

Sugar Crackers.
Louisa C. Light.

1 pound of sugar, ½ pound of butter, ½ cup of sour cream, ½ teaspoon of baking soda put in the sour cream, 1 teaspoonful cinnamon, 1 teaspoonful cloves, ½ teaspoonful allspice.

Oatmeal Crackers.
Mrs. J. K. Fisher.

2 cups of brown sugar, 2 cups of rolled oat meal, 1 scant cup of butter and lard, 2 scant teaspoons of soda in 1 cup of hot water; flour enough to make stiff. Roll very thin, cut in squares, place on tins and bake in a good oven.

Good Bread.
Mrs. Joseph Southam.

To make good bread take about 9 pounds of flour, then make a large well in the flour, then add 1 quart and pint of warm water and stir until stiff; add cup of yeast; stir well and let raise over night; in the morning add 3 handfuls granulated sugar, 1 handful of salt, teaspoon of lard, and knead ¾ hour.

Peptik Bread.
Mrs. Blanche McNeal.

1 quart flour, 1 teaspoonful salt, 2 teaspoonfuls of Cleveland baking powder, 1 pint of cold water or milk. Mix the flour, salt and baking powder thoroughly, then make a well in the center and pour into this all the water; be sure and use enough water to make the dough quite soft. Stir quickly and thoroughly together and when the dough is wet stir a moment longer, then turn at once into a well greased baking pan; the pan should be about 4 inches wide, 4 inches deep and 8 inches long. After the dough is in the pan smooth the top with a knife dipped in melted butter. Bake at once for 1 hour in a moderate oven; when finished remove from the pan, sprinkle with water and wrap in a bread cloth until cool. This bread is especially recommended to those of weak digestion.

Cottolene requires only 2-3 the quantity of lard. Use it.

ICINGS.

Filling for Cake.
Mrs. R. E. U.

2 oranges, grated; 1 cup sugar, 1 tablespoonful corn starch, a scant cup of water; boil until clear; cool before putting between the cake.

Boiled Icing.
Mrs. D. Rodearmel.

2 cups sugar, whites of 2 eggs, 1 cup rolled peanuts, ½ cup English walnuts, ½ cup seedless raisins.

Chocolate Icing.

Melt 2 squares (¼ cake) chocolate in ¼ cup hot water; stir in confectioner's sugar till thick enough to spread; keep warm, but do not boil; add 1 teaspoonful vanilla extract; stir until smooth.

Water Icing.

Take any quantity of powdered sugar you may require, add cold water enough to make a thick paste (it will not take much). Flavor.

Chocolate Frosting.
Mrs. D. M. Karmany.

3 tablespoonfuls grated chocolate, ½ cup sugar, a little water. Boil until thick.

Filling for Layer Cake.
Mrs. I M. Hean.

Boil ½ pint of milk, thicken with corn starch, add the yolks of 2 eggs, reserving the whites for top of cake; flavor with orange or vanilla, and sweeten to taste.

Chocolate Icing, Boiled.
Mrs. J. H. Roberts.

½ cake of chocolate, 1 cup of white sugar, ½ cup of sweet nearly a pound; let the milk and egg come to a boil, then add the egg. Remove from fire and pour over chocolate.

Chocolate Icing.
Mrs. John T. Atkins.

½ cake of chocolatae, 1 cup of whiet sugar, ½ cup of sweet milk, yolk of 1 egg, after boiled; flavor with vanilla.

Shellbark Icing.
Mrs. Morris Weidman.

2 cups of white sugar, add ¾ cup of water, boil until it ropes; do not stir while boiling; beat until thick, then add 2 tablespoonfuls of grated chocolate; spread on the cake; have ready 1 cup of chopped shellbark kernels and sprinkle over the icing.

White Boiled Icing.
Mrs. J. H. Roberts.

1 pound granulated sugar, 2 tablespoons vinegar, ½ cup cold water, whites of 2 eggs; flavor to taste. Let the sugar, water and vinegar boil until stringy; flavor; add the whites and remove from the fire; beat until stiff enough for the cake.

Chocolate Icing.

Whites of 3 eggs, well beaten; ½ cake of chocolate (Baker's), steamed over the tea-kettle; pulverized sugar enough to sweeten to taste; flavor with vanilla.

Lemon Icing.

Juice and rind of 1 lemon, 1 egg, 3 tablespoonfuls of water, 1 small cup sugar; mix well together, boil until clear and thick.

Walnut Filling.
Mrs. K. H. Mish.

1 cup of English walnuts, chopped fine; 1 cup raisins, seeded and chopped fine; 1 cup sugar, 1 tablespoon of prepared cocoanut, white of 1 egg; place sugar on fire with water enough to prevent burning; when melted add ingredients and boil 3 minutes, then add the beaten white of the egg; spread on cake at once.

Marshmallow Filling.
Mrs. F. P. Spiese, Tamaqua.

4 eggs, ½ cup of water, 2 cups of sugar, 2 cups of flour, 2 teaspoonfuls of Cleveland baking powder; beat the yolks and

sugar as for sponge cake, then add water, the whites which have been beaten stiff, and the flour. For filling—2 tablespoonfuls gelatine, dissolved in ¾ cup of warm water; 1 pound of pulverized sugar; beat sugar and gelatine about ½ hour; flavor with 1 teaspoonful of vanilla or 2 tablespoonfuls of cocoa or chocolate.

JAMS, JELLIES, ETC.

Currant Jam.

2 pounds ripe currants, 1 pound currant juice, 3 pounds raisins, seeded, 4 pounds sugar, 1 dozen oranges, chopped. Mix all together and stew over a slow fire.

Blackberry Jam.

2 quarts mashed blackberries, 1 quart apple sauce, 1 quart sugar. Cook 20 minutes.

Red Raspberries With Currants.

3 quarts red raspberries, 1 quart currants. Jam together and allow a pound of sugar for a pound of fruit. Stir well together and cook ½ an hour.

Grape Jam.

Take any quantity of grapes and remove pulp from the skin. Boil a few minutes, and strain through a sieve to take out the seeds. Then add the skins. For 1 pound of this use ¾ of a pound of sugar. Boil until it thickens.

Quince Jelly.

Peel and cut up ripe quinces. Cover with cold water and stew until soft. Strain, and boil the juice 20 minutes. Allow nearly 1 pound of sugar to 1 of fruit. Add the hot sugar, and only let it boil a moment—until it jellies from the spoon.

Spiced Plums.

To 8 pounds of plums allow 4 pounds of sugar; 1 teaspoon each of cinnamon and cloves, 1 small cup of vinegar.

Jelly

Cook the fruit with as little water as possible, according to the fruit. Put in cheese cloth or flannel bags and let it drain over night. Next morning put juice in the kettle, after measuring. At the same time measure your sugar and put in the oven. Let the fruit juice boil about 20 minutes, add the hot sugar and the jelly will be ready to put in glasses immediately, and will be much clearer than if boiled after sugar is put in. Set your jelly glasses on a cloth, wet with cold water and they will not break filling.

Apple Jelly.

Boil and strain the apples. To 1 pint of juice add nearly 1 pint of hot sugar. Flavor by passing a rose geranium leaf through the jelly just before taking from the fire. This makes a delicate and nice jelly, but the leaf must not stay in long.

Grape Jelly.

Jelly is nicer made with green grapes than ripe. Mash with a potato masher and strain. 1 pint of juice to 1 pint of sugar. Boil the juice 20 minutes and add the sugar. Boil until it jellies.

Pineapple.

Chop or grate the pineapple. Allow 1 cup of fruit to 1 cup of sugar, and cook slowly 20 minutes, or until tender. The grated pineapple is very nice to put between layers of cake, and to make desserts.

Spiced Peaches.

3 pounds sugar to 1 pint vinegar. Boil and skim before putting in the peaches. Pare the peaches and cook until tender. Can in glass jars and seal. Peaches can easily be pared by dropping them in hot water with a little lye in it. But if pared with a knife the skins can be used for butter or marmalade.

Pickled Pears.

1 quart water, 1 pint good strong vinegar, $\frac{1}{2}$ pound sugar, some cassia buds. When this boils, add as many prepared pears as the syrup will just cover. Boil slowly until tender and then can.

BISCUITS, BUNS, ETC.

Blueberry Tea Cake.

3 cups huckleberries, 2 tablespoons butter, 2 teaspoons Cleveland baking powder, 1 cup sugar, 1 cup milk, 3 cups flour; cream butter and sugar, add milk, flour and baking powder; stir in the berries, after dredging with flour, and bake the cake on biscuit tins. To be buttered and eaten hot.

Crumb Griddle Cakes.
Mrs. F. P. Spiese, Tamaqua.

Soak 1 pint of dry bread crumbs in sweet milk over night; in the morning take 1½ cups of sour milk, ½ teaspoonful of soda, a little salt, and wheat flour to make a thin batter.

Soda Biscuit.
Mrs. M. Katzenberg.

2 quarts of flour, 1 pint of sweet milk, ½ cup butter or lard, 3 teaspoonfuls of Cleveland baking powder.

Boston Corn Bread.
Mrs. J. I. Stahr, Lancaster.

1 cup sweet milk, 2 cups sour milk, 2-3 cup molasses, 1 cup flour, 4 cups corn-meal, 2 teaspoons soda. Steam 3 hours and brown a few moments in oven.

Corn Muffins.

1 quart milk, ¾ pound corn-meal, ½ pound butter and lard mixed, ½ pound sugar, 5 eggs, 2 pounds flour, 1½ ounces cream of tartar, ¾ ounce of carbonate of soda; mix all ingredients, except milk and eggs, which must be added last. If baked in gem pans use prescribed quantity of cream of tartar and soda; if not, use less. For a small family the recipe must be reduced.

Rice Waffles.

¾ pint of milk, 1 pint boiled rice, 1 pint flour, 2 eggs, 1 teaspoon salt, butter, the size of an egg; 2 teaspoons Cleveland baking powder.

Cottolene requires only 2-3 the quantity of lard. Use it.

Muffins.
Mrs. J. K. Fisher.

Sift 1 quart of flour and 3 teaspoons of baking powder together, add a teaspoon of salt, 1 pint of sweet milk, 2 eggs, beaten separately; ½ cup of melted butter; drop into puff pans or rings that have been well greased with butter, and thoroughly heated; much depends upon a good hot oven.

Corn Cakes.
H. M. M.

2 cups of corn-meal, 1 cup of wheat flour, 1 teaspoon of salt, 1 teaspoon of sugar; mix with thick milk 1 egg separate, and beat the white stiff; put in last; scald the soda and put in mixture. Fry in an inch of lard.

Corn Griddle Cakes.
Miss Emma G. Scott.

2 cups of corn-meal, 1 cup of flour, 1 teaspoonful brown sugar, ½ teaspoonful of salt, 2 teaspoonfuls Cleveland baking powder, 2 eggs, 1 pint of milk. Sift together corn-meal, flour, salt, sugar and powder, add beaten eggs and milk, mix into a smooth batter. Bake on a very hot griddle to a nice brown.

Corn Bread.
Mrs. James Scott.

1½ cups of sour cream, ½ cup of butter, ½ cup of sugar, 1 cup of flour, 2 cups of corn-meal, 1 teaspoonful of soda, ½ teaspoonful of salt, 1 egg. Put all in together and beat until light. Bake 35 minutes in a hot oven and serve hot.

Waffles.

Sift 2 teaspoonfuls of Cleveland baking powder into 1 quart of flour; rub into it 1-3 cup of butter; add sweet milk enough to make a batter; add 3 eggs and a little salt.

Tea Buns.
Mrs. John Urich.

1 cup of yeast, 1 cup of mashed potatoes, 1 cup of sugar. Let stand over night; in the morning stir in 1 cup of sweet milk, 1 cup of shortening, 1 egg, a little salt. Knead like bread; when raised form into rolls.

Cottolene requires only 2-3 the quantity of lard. Use it.

Lebanon Rusk.
Mrs. J. S. Stahr, Lancaster.

1 cup mashed potatoes, 1 cup sugar, 1 of home-made yeast, 3 eggs; mix together; when raised light, add $\frac{1}{2}$ cup butter or lard, and flour to make a soft dough, and when quite light mould into small cakes and let rise again before baking. If wanted for tea set about 9 a. m.

Spanish Buns.
Mrs. Jos. Krause.

3 eggs, well beaten; 1$\frac{1}{2}$ cups of sugar, $\frac{1}{4}$ pound of butter; beat the three together; 4 cups of flour, 3 teaspoonfuls Cleveland baking powder, $\frac{1}{2}$ pound of currants, 2 cups of sweet milk.

Potato Buns.
Mrs. James Scott.

Set in the evening a cup of potato water, a cup of sugar, and a cup of yeast, with a cup of mashed potatoes. Add in the morning a cup of sugar, a cup of lard or butter, and 1 egg, with flour to stiffen. Roll to a thickness of about $\frac{1}{2}$ an inch, and cut with an ordinary cutter. After placing in the pans, allow them to rise until light, then bake in a moderate oven about 25 minutes.

Parker House Rolls.
Mrs. S. Y. Karmany.

Set in the morning at 9 o'clock, 3 pints of flour, 1 pint sweet milk, teaspoon of salt, 1 tablespoon sugar, 3 eggs, well beaten; 1 cake of yeast, $\frac{3}{4}$ cup of butter. Heat the milk sufficient to melt the butter; when milk becomes lukewarm mix in the flour. After all the ingredients are in, then add yeast; stir with spoon at 1 o'clock; do not knead. At 4.30 remove from the bowl, flatten on board and cut out 1 inch thick; rub with melted butter and turn over to shape the roll. Let rise and bake.

Tea Biscuit.
Mrs. W. H. Newhard, Allentown.

1 quart flour, 1 tablespoonful of lard, a little salt, 4 heaping teaspoonfuls Cleveland baking powder, well sifted in the flour; sweet milk enough to mix..

Cottolene requires only 2-3 the quantity of lard. Use it.

BISCUITS, BUNS, ETC.

Entire Wheat Gems.
Dr. Alice B. Stockham.

Take 3 cups of entire wheat flour or graham made from white wheat, 2 cups of cold water, ½ cup of milk; a little more wetting may be needed for graham. Omit salt. Heat gem pans very hot on the top of the stove, fill them even full with the batter, place them on the grate of a very hot oven; let them remain 10 minutes, then bake 30 minutes on the bottom of the oven. The "acorn" gem pans are essential. These are small, round, deep iron pans. Notice—Three things are necessary for good gems: The best entire wheat flour, very hot pans and oven, and the "acorn" gem pans. No beating is required. These conditions observed, the gems will be light as sponge cake. They can be eaten warm or cold, but are best heated over in a quick oven. They make excellent toast and pudding. I was many years learning to make good gems without yeast or soda. This recipe never fails, even with a "green" cook.

Graham Gems.
Mrs. A. G. Banks, Middletown.

1 pint butter-milk, 1 teaspoonful soda, 1 egg, 3 tablespoonfuls sugar, 1 tablespoonful lard, a little salt; thicken with graham flour and bake in gem tins.

Parker House Rolls.
Mrs. J. Karch.

1½ quarts of sifted flour, 1 pint of warm milk, butter, the size of an egg; 1 tablespoonful of sugar, 1 egg, pinch of salt, 1 cake of Fleichman's yeast. Let the sponge rise for a few hours, then knead stiff, and let rise again; when ready, cut out for rolls. Bake a light brown.

Paper Biscuit.
Mrs. Ella D. Moore.

1 pound butter, 1 pound sugar, 3 eggs; flour to stiffen.

French Loaf.

4 cups of butter, 6 cups of sugar, 3 cups of milk, 10 cups of flour, 8 eggs, 2 pounds of raisins, 1 pound of currants, ½ pound of citron; use flavor that is preferred; 1 teaspoonful of soda.

Cottolene requires only 2-3 the quantity of lard. Use it.

Potato Puffs.
Mrs. R. S. Malsberger.

2 cups of cold mashed potatoes, 2 eggs, well beaten; ½ cup of cream or milk, scant ½ cup of flour, with 1 teaspoonful of Cleveland baking powder, a little grated onion, salt and pepper; beat all well together and drop, a tablespoonful at a time, in hot lard as you would crullers.

Scotch Scones.
Fannie Atkins.

1 quart of flour, 1 teaspoon of sugar, ½ teaspoon of salt, 2 teaspoons of Cleveland baking powder, nearly 1 pint of sweet milk, 1 large tablespoon of lard, 2 eggs. Sift together flour, baking powder, sugar and salt, rub in the lard, then add the beaten eggs and milk; mix into a smooth dough; turn out the dough on a bake board and give it two good kneadings; roll out 1-3 inch in thickness, cut in squares larger than a soda cracker; fold each in half to form three-cornered pieces. Bake at once.

Quick Waffles.
H. M. M.

1 pint of milk, 3 eggs, beaten light; 1 tablespoon of melted butter, 1 tablespoon of cream of tartar, ½ teaspoon of soda, 1 teaspoon of salt, heaping pint of flour.

Butter Biscuit.
Mrs. Klopp.

1 pound of sugar, 1 pound of butter, 3 eggs, 1 pint of sweet milk, 2 teaspoonfuls Cleveland baking powder.

Biscuits.
Mrs. Jos. Krause.

Scald 1 pint sweet milk, add 1 large tablespoonful butter, 2 large tablespoonfuls sugar, ½ yeast cake. When sponge is light, make a soft dough. let rise until morning, then work and put in pans; let rise an hour, then bake.

Corn Cakes.
Mrs. Pitcher, Jackson, Mo.

1 quart corn-meal, 1 quart sour milk, 1 egg, 1 teaspoon soda, 1 of salt. Bake on griddle.

Cottolene requires only 2-3 the quantity of lard. Use it.

Dutch Loaf.
Mrs. John T. Atkins.

1 cup of potatoes, 1 cup of yeast, 1 cup of sugar; let stand all night; add 1 cup of sugar 1 cup of lard and butter, 1 cup of sweet milk, 2 eggs; knead stiff.

Corn Pone.
Mrs. M. Katzenberg.

2 cups of corn-meal, 1 cup of white flour, 3 eggs, 1 cup sugar, ½ cup melted butter, 1 teaspoon salt, 2 heaping teaspoonfuls of Cleveland baking powder, 1 cup of sweet milk

Indian Pound Cake.
Anna M. Hammer.

¾ pound of sugar, 6 ounces of butter, 6 eggs, weight of 5 eggs in meal; separate the eggs and beat well; add juice and grated rind of 1 lemon, and beat in the Indian meal last. Bake in quick oven; when turned out of the pan, spread well with currant jelly, while the cake is warm.

Sallie Lunn.

Beat yolks of 2 eggs, 2 tablespoons sugar and ½ cup butter together until light, add cup milk and enough flour to make a stiff cake batter; beat smooth; add whites of eggs beaten to a stiff froth and 1 heaping teaspoon baking powder. Bake in greased cake pan (with cylinder) for ¾ of an hour in moderate oven. Serve hot.

Fruit Pinwheels.
Mrs. J. C. Urich, Marquette, Mich.

Mix together and rub through sieve the following mixture: 1 pint flour, 1 tablespoon sugar, ½ teaspoon salt, 2 teaspoons Cleveland baking powder; into this rub 2 heaping tablespoons butter, wet with scant ½ pint milk; sprinkle board with flour, roll into large squares ½ inch thick, spread with heaping tablespoon soft butter, also, 1 cup sugar, 1 cup currants; grate nutmeg over all, and roll up like jelly rolls, cut in slices ¾ inch thick, lay in well buttered pans and bake in hot oven.

Cottolene requires only 2-3 the quantity of lard. Use it.

SMALL CAKES.

Sand Tarts.
Esther J. Boyer.

1 pound sugar, 1 pound flour, 2 eggs, 10 ounces butter; work sugar and butter to a cream, then add the rest; keep a portion of the eggs out to put on top of the cakes after they are rolled out. Wash them with the egg, sprinkle sugar and cinnamon on top, also add a shellbark.

Sand Tarts.
Mary L. Graeff.

2 pounds sugar, 1 pound butter, 2 pounds flour, 5 eggs; mix flour and sugar; add butter and eggs, beaten thoroughly.

Sand Tarts.
Mrs. Paine.

1 pound of sugar, 3 eggs, 1 cup of butter; use flour enough to roll.

Sand Tarts.
Mrs. Amanda H. Fry, Pleasant Grove.

Rub 1 pound of butter into 2 pounds of flour, then add 2 pounds of sugar; wet the whole with 3 eggs, well beaten; roll thin and cut.

Sand Tarts.
Miss Mary Stover.

2 pounds of flour, $1\frac{1}{4}$ pounds of butter; rub together; add 2 pounds of sugar, 3 eggs, beaten light; wash with egg; when in the pan sprinkle with sugar, cinnamon and nuts.

Sand Tarts.
E. Seltzer.

1 pound sugar, 1 pound flour, 6 ounces butter, 2 eggs.

Plain Cookies.
Elma Fry, Pleasant Grove.

2 cups sugar, 1 cup butter, 1 cup sweet milk, 5 cups flour, 2 eggs, 4 teaspoons Cleveland baking powder; drop or roll thin; bake quickly.

SMALL CAKES.

Cookies.

1 pound sugar, 3¼ cups butter, 5 eggs, 1 teaspoon soda in the flour; make dough just stiff enough to roll.

Eggless Cookies.

1 pound soft white sugar, 1 cup butter, (or ½ cup butter and ½ cup lard) 2-3 pint thick milk, 1 teaspoon soda; flour enough to roll out moderately stiff; flavor with cinnamon and grated nutmeg.

Chocolate Cookies.
Mrs. S. Reinoehl.

9 tablespoonfuls flour, 2 tablespoonfuls lard, 2 tablespoonfuls butter, ½ pound sugar, ¼ pound grated chocolate, 1 teaspoonful soda, 1 teaspoonful cinnamon, also cloves; moisten with 2 eggs. Roll very thin.

Woolover's Cookies.

3 eggs, 2 cups sugar, 1 cup butter, ½ cup sour cream or milk; 2 even teaspoons soda, nutmeg to flavor, and flour to stiffen.

Walnut Cookies.
Mrs. J. Dewald.

1 pound of sugar, 1 pound of nuts, 3 eggs, 3 tablespoons flour. Both the white and yellow of the eggs.

Ginger Cake.
Mrs. David Harpel.

3 eggs, 1 cup sugar, (beat together) add 1 cup molasses, ¾ cup lard, 1 tablespoon ginger, 1 tablespoon soda, dissolve in a little boiling water and stir in; 4 cups flour; beat well together then pour in 1 cup boiling water. Bake in a slow oven.

Ginger Cake.
Mrs. Moore, Indianapolis, Ind.

1 cup of sugar, 1 cup of butter, 1 cup of molasses, 1 cup of milk, 4 eggs, 1 teaspoonful of cream of tartar, 1 tablespoonful of ginger, 1 teaspoonful of soda, 4 cups of flour.

Cocoanut Drops.
Mrs. J. H. Roberts.

1 pound of sugar, ½ pound butter, 2 eggs, 1 cocoanut, grated; flour enough to drop on tins.

Cottolene requires only 2-3 the quantity of lard. Use it.

SMALL CAKES.

Sugar Cakes.
Mrs. John B. Fisher, Lancaster.

2 pounds of sugar, 1 tincup of butter and lard, 2 cups of thick milk, 4 eggs, 3 scant pounds of flour, 1 tablespoon of soda, 1 teaspoon of cream of tartar.

Sugar Cakes.
Mrs. S. R. Kendall.

3 pounds of sugar, ¾ pounds of butter, 1 quart of sour milk, 1 tablespoon of soda. Flour stiff enough for spoon to stick in without dropping over.

A. P.'s.

3 eggs, well beaten; ½ cup of butter, ½ cup of cream, ½ pound white sugar, ½ teaspoonful soda, ½ teaspoonful cream of tartar. Roll out thin.

A. P.'s.
Mrs. R. G. Stanley.

1 pound granulated sugar, ½ pound of butter, 3 eggs, ½ cup sour cream, ½ teaspoon of soda; flour to stiffen. Roll thin.

Drop Cakes.

2 pounds sugar, ¾ pound butter, 6 eggs, 2½ cups sour milk, 1 scant tablespoon soda, 1 teaspoon cream of tartar.

Lemon Cakes.
Mrs. A. M. Thomas.

3 tablespoons flour, 1 cup sugar, 1 quart boiling water; scald 1 lemon, 3 eggs, butter, size of walnut, pinch of salt.

Cocoanut Drops.
Mrs. Ira Rutter.

1½ pounds flour, 6 ounces butter, 1 pound brown sugar, 1 pint N. O. molasses, boiled; 1 grated cocoanut. Drop them.

Cocoanut Drops.

½ pound grated cocoanut, ½ pound loaf sugar, whites of 3 eggs; drop on buttered paper and bake.

Cocoanut Drops.

2 grated cocoanuts, an equal weight of sugar, whites of 3 eggs, well beaten; make size of a dollar, and bake on buttered tins.

Cottolene requires only 2-3 the quantity of lard. Use it.

Chocolate Cake.
Hattie Bickel.

½ pound butter, ½ pound sugar, ½ pound flour, ½ cake chocolate, 1 teaspoon Cleveland baking powder, 1 teaspoon cinnamon, 1 teaspoon cloves, 2 eggs.

Molasses Cakes.
Mrs. Dr. Deckert.

1 pint molasses, 1 pound brown sugar, 1 cup of shortening, 1 cup sweet milk, 1 tablespoon soda. Work the sugar and butter and put the soda in the molasses, then mix with flour.

Molasses Cakes.

1 quart molasses, 1 cup of thick milk, 1 tablespoon soda; flour to stiffen; spices to taste.

Molasses Cakes.
Mrs. John T. Atkins.

1 quart of New Orleans molasses, cup of sour milk, ½ pint of lard, 2 tablespoons of soda, cloves and ginger.

Honey Cakes.
Mrs. A. M. Thomas.

1 cup sugar, 1 cup New Orleans molasses, 1 egg, 1 teaspoon soda, 1 tablespoon vinegar.

Molasses Cakes.
Mrs. Mallman.

1 quart of molasses, 1 cup of sugar, 1½ cups of thick milk, 1 cup of lard, 1 tablespoonful of ginger, 1 tablespoonful of cinnamon, 2 tablespoonfuls of baking soda stirred in the milk; flour enough to roll.

Taylor Cakes.
Mrs. Ira Rutter.

1 pint New Orleans molasses, 1 cup sugar, 1 cup butter and lard, ½ pint sour milk, 3 eggs, a little salt, 1 tablespoon of soda, nutmeg, cloves and cinnamon. Flour enough to drop.

Drop Cakes.
Mrs. Ebright.

1 cup of sweet milk, 3 cups of sugar, ¾ cup of lard, 4 cups of flour, 3 eggs, 2 teaspoons powder.

Cottolene requires only 2-3 the quantity of lard. Use it.

Drop Cakes.
Mrs. R. S. Malsberger.

5 eggs, 1 cup sour cream, 2 cups sugar, ½ cup butter, 5 cups flour, 1 teaspoonful soda, 2 teaspoonfuls cream of tartar.

Ginger Drop Cakes.

1 cup butter, scant; 1 cup sugar, 1 cup molasses, 3 eggs, 1 tablespoon of soda, dissolved in a cup of boiling water; 1 teaspoon each of cinnamon, ginger, and cloves; 5 cups of flour.

Drop Cakes.
Mrs. A. M. Thomas.

3 cups sugar, 4 eggs, 1 cup butter and lard, 1 cup sour milk, 4 cups flour, 2 teaspoons Cleveland baking powder.

Molasses Drop Cakes.
Mrs. Reese.

1 cup of molasses, 3 cups of flour, ½ cup of butter, 2 teaspoonfuls of extract of lemon, and 1 teaspoonful of baking soda. Beat the ingredients together thoroughly and drop in spoonfuls upon buttered tins. Bake 5 or 6 minutes.

Drop Cakes.
Mrs. R. H. Graeff.

6 cups flour, 3 cups sugar, 2 cups butter, 3 eggs, flavor with nutmeg and drop on tins.

Kisses.

Whites of 3 eggs, beaten stiff; add gradually 1 pound sifted, powdered sugar, flavor with vanilla; drop on buttered tins; bake in a moderate oven.

Walnut Cakes.
Mrs. Amelia Ohlwiler, Altoona.

1 pound sugar, 4 tablespoons of flour, the whites of 6 eggs, beat sugar and eggs to an icing, crumb in 1 pound of walnut kernels, drop on tins and bake slowly.

Nut Cakes.
Mrs. H. B. Greiner.

1 pound sugar, 1 pound nuts (shellbarks), 4 eggs, 2 tablespoonfuls flour; beat the whites of eggs last; drop on tin with teaspoon.

Cottolene requires only 2-3 the quantity of lard. Use it.

Pepper Nuts.
Mrs. Robert Hean.

1 pound sugar, 4 eggs, 1 cup cream, 1 cup butter, 1 teaspoon salaratus, 1 teaspoon pepper.

Pepper Nuts.
Mrs. Englehart.

1 pound of sugar, 1 cup of butter, 3 eggs, 1 cup of sour milk, 1 teaspoonful of soda; make soft dough to roll out.

Pepper Nuts.
Mrs. E. Michael.

¾ pound of butter, 1¼ pounds of sugar, 3 eggs, 1 cup sour milk, rose water or essence of lemon to taste, flour enough to roll out, 2 small teaspoonfuls of cream of tartar and 1 of soda.

Tea Cakes.
Mrs. Rev. I. C. Fisher.

2 cups of sugar, 1 cup of butter, 1 cup of sour cream, 3 eggs, 1 teaspoon of soda and cream of tartar; flour enough to roll out; sprinkle with granulated sugar.

Tea Cakes.
Esther J. Boyer.

1 pound sugar, 1 cup butter, 3 eggs, ½ nutmeg, 1 teaspoonful baking soda, 1 teaspoonful cream of tartar, ⅓ up thick milk; not too stiff with flour.

Farmers Doughnuts.
Ella Houseman.

1 egg, cup of thick milk, or more; 1 teaspoon of soda; flour to thicken, to be dipped with a spoon. Fry same as doughnuts in lard.

Doughnuts.
Mrs. Jenks, Bellefontaine, Ohio.

1 egg, 1 cup rich milk, 1 cup sugar, flour enough to roll out, 3 teaspoons of Cleveland baking powder.

Fasnacht Cakes.
Mrs. John B. Fisher, Lancaster.

1 cup of yeast, 1 cup of melted lard, 1 cup of sugar, 4 large potatoes (mashed dry) in yeast, 1 tincup of water, salt to taste. Roll out thin, cut to suit and swim in hot lard.

Cottolene requires only 2-3 the quantity of lard. Use it.

Doughnuts.
Mrs. R. E. U.

1 cup sweet milk, 1 egg, 1 handful sugar, 1 tablespoon half butter and half lard, 2 teaspoons Cleveland baking powder, a pinch of salt; mix soft; roll out and fry in hot lard. (Very good.)

Doughnuts.
Mrs. M. Katzenberg.

1 pint thick milk, 3 cupfuls of sugar, 7 tablespoonfuls of lard, 2 eggs, 1 teaspoonful of soda, 2 teaspoonfuls of cream of tartar. Flour to make soft.

Doughnuts.
Mrs. Scott, Indianapolis, Ind.

2 cups of sugar, 1 cup of sweet milk, 1 egg, 3 teaspoonfuls Cleveland baking powder, $\frac{1}{2}$ teaspoonful of salt, nutmeg or other spice.

Molasses Cookies.
Mrs. E. P. Werley, Allentown, Pa.

1 quart New Orleans molasses, $\frac{3}{4}$ cup lard, 1 ounce soda, 1 cup thick milk; flour to stiffen, and let stand over night; beat white of 1 egg and spread on top of cakes before baking.

Ginger Cookies.

1 cup sugar, 1 cup molasses, 1 cup of lard, 1 egg, 2 teaspoonfuls of soda, $\frac{1}{2}$ cup of warm water, tablespoonful of ginger, a little salt; roll as soft as you can.

Molasses Cookies.

1 quart molasses, 1 small pint sour milk, 1 small pint of melted butter and lard, 2 tablespoonfuls of soda, 1 teaspoonful of cream of tartar, 1 tablespoonful of ginger.

Ginger Snaps.
Mrs. S. E. Breslin.

1 cup warm molasses, $1\frac{1}{2}$ cups sugar, 1 egg, 1 cup of butter, 1 teaspoon of soda, 5 cups of flour, 2 tablespoons of ginger.

Hickorynut Cookies.

1 egg, $\frac{1}{2}$ cup flour, 1 cup sugar, 1 cup nuts, chopped fine; drop on buttered tins, 1 teaspoonful in a place, 2 inches apart.

Cottolene requires only 2-3 the quantity of lard. Use it.

Ginger Cookies.

1 teaspoonful of ginger, 1 cup butter and lard mixed, 1 cup sugar, 1 cup common black molasses, 2 eggs, pinch of salt, 1 tablespoonful of salaratus, dissolved in 4 tablespoonfuls of vinegar; flour to make stiff.

Ginger Cakes.
Mrs. John B. Fisher, Lancaster.

10 ounces of butter and lard, ½ pint of thick milk, 1 ounce of soda, ginger, cloves and cinnamon, 3 pounds flour, 1 quart of New Orleans molasses.

Hickorynut Cookies.
Mrs. Ella D. Moore.

1 cup sugar, 4 tablespoons flour, 2 cups kernels, cut fine, 2 eggs. Drop on tins.

Ginger Cakes.
Mrs. S. S. Herr, Pleasant Grove.

1 quart New Orleans molasses, 1¾ cups melted lard, 1 cup boiling water, ½ cup sugar, 2 tablespoonfuls ginger, 3 tablespoonfuls soda; flour to make a soft dough.

Ginger Snaps.
Mrs. K. H. Mish.

2 cups molasses, 1 cup sugar, 4 tablespoonfuls of water, 1 cup butter, 2 tablespoonfuls ginger, 1 teaspoonful cinnamon, cloves and allspice each, 1 teaspoonful soda, 8 cups flour.

Ginger Snaps.
Mrs. S. B. Cox.

1 pint of molasses, a small ½ pint of lard, 1 tablespoonful of ginger, 1 tablespoonful of soda, and enough flour to make it very stiff.

Ginger Snaps.
Mrs. Beyerle.

3 pints of flour, 1 large cup of lard or butter, mixed together same as pie crust; 1 cup of brown sugar, 1 tablespoonful ginger, 1 teaspoonful of cinnamon, 1 of cloves, a little nutmeg, 1 teaspoonful of cream of tartar, 1 teaspoonful of soda, 1 pint of baking molasses. Knead into a stiff dough and roll thin; cut and bake.

Cottolene requires only 2-3 the quantity of lard. Use it.

SMALL CAKES.

Ginger Snaps.
Mrs. H. A. Spiese, Tamaqua.

1 cup brown sugar, 1 cup New Orleans molasses, 1 cup lard, 1 teaspoonful of soda, and a pinch of salt. Put molasses, sugar, lard and soda on the stove to boil, then pour over the flour and spices, mixing them thoroughly, and let cool. Take 5 cups of flour, 1 teaspoonful of cloves, 1 teaspoonful of allspice, 1 teaspoonful of cinnamon and 2 teaspoonfuls of ginger.

Chocolate Snaps.
Mrs. F. P. Spiese, Tamaqua.

1 egg, 2 cups of brown sugar, $\frac{1}{2}$ cup butter, 1 cup grated chocolate, $\frac{1}{2}$ cup milk, $\frac{1}{2}$ teaspoonful baking soda; flour enough to roll. Must be rolled thin and baked in a quick oven.

Ginger Snaps.
Mrs. Foster.

Boil 5 minutes 1 pint molasses, 1 teacup butter, 1 tablespoon each of ginger, cloves and cinnamon. Roll very thin.

Small Chocolate Cake.

3 cups of brown sugar, $\frac{3}{4}$ cup of butter and lard $\frac{1}{2}$ cup thick milk, 1 cup of chocolate, $1\frac{1}{2}$ teaspoons of soda, $1\frac{1}{2}$ teaspoons of cream of tartar. Flour to stiffen.

Little Ring Cakes.
Mrs. F. P. Spiese, Tamaqua.

14 ounces of sugar, 1 pound of flour, 3-8 pound of butter, yolks of 5 eggs, 1 teaspoonful of soda; put into the flour dry or mixed with a little milk; cut in small rings. Wash the top with the yolk of an egg, sprinkle with cinnamon and sugar, and bake.

Jumbles.
Mrs. J. Karch.

1 pound sugar, 1 pound flour, 3 eggs, $\frac{1}{2}$ pound butter, $\frac{1}{2}$ teaspoon soda.

Jumbles.
Mrs. F.

1 pound sugar, $\frac{3}{4}$ pound butter, 1 pound flour, 3 eggs, $\frac{1}{2}$ teaspoon soda.

Cottolene requires only 2-3 the quantity of lard. Use it.

Jumbles.
Mrs. Ella D. Moore.

2 pounds flour, 1 pound butter, 1 pound sugar, 3 eggs, 1 cup sour cream, ½ teaspoonful of baking soda, 1 teaspoonful of cream of tartar.

Jumbles.
Mrs. Amanda H. Fry, Pleasant Grove.

1 pound of sugar, 1 pound of butter, 2 pounds of flour, 2 eggs, 1 teaspoon of soda; take as much sweet cream as will make it stick together; work flour and butter together first.

Chocolate Jumbles.
Mrs. Rev. A. M. Stirk, Allentown.

1 cup of butter, 2 cups of sugar, 3½ cups of flour, 1 cup of grated chocolate, 4 eggs, 1 teaspoon of soda, 1 teaspoon of cream of tartar, cream, butter and sugar.

Cocoanut Jumbles.
Mrs. John H. Diehl.

1 pound sugar, 1 pound flour, 1 cup butter, 1 grated cocoanut, ½ cup sweet milk, 4 eggs, 1 teaspoon Cleveland baking powder; if too soft, add a little more flour.

Lemon Jumbles.

1 pound of flour, 1 pound of sugar, 5-8 pound of butter, 4 eggs, the juice and rind of 1 lemon, and as little flour as will enable you to make the whole into small cakes with your hands.

Cocoanut Jumbles.
Mrs. H. A. Spiese, Tamaqua.

1 pound white sugar, ¼ pound butter, 1¼ pounds flour, 4 eggs, ½ teaspoonful soda, 1 teaspoonful cream of tartar, 1 cocoanut, grated; roll in sugar.

Poplar Chips.
Mrs. John B. Fisher, Lancaster.

1 tincup of sweet milk, 3 eggs, 3 tablespoonfuls of melted lard, salt to taste, ½ teaspoonful of soda; roll very thin; cut in chips and swim in hot lard.

PICKLES.

"Peter Piper picked a peck of pickled peppers."

Chow Chow.
M. M. B.

¼ peck small string beans, ¼ peck tomatoes, ½ dozen green peppers, ¼ dozen red peppers, 1 quart small white onions, 3 dozen ears of sugar corn, 2 dozen very small cucumbers, 1 head cauliflower, ¼ pound white mustard seed, ¼ pound black mustard seed, 1 tablespoon of celery seed, 2 tablespoonfuls of tumeric powder, 2 tablespoons of salad oil. Salt beans, tomatoes, peppers, and onions under pressure for 12 hours. Mix well together; boil 1 hour in cider vinegar; add oil and tumeric powder last.

Chow Chow.
Mrs. James Scott.

1 peck green tomatoes, ½ peck onions, 2 dozen peppers, 2 heads of cabbage; chop fine and mix all together and salt it. Place it in a bag to drain over night. Then add ¼ pound of mustard seed, ½ ounce whole cloves, ½ ounce cinnamon, ½ ounce mace, 2 pounds brown sugar; cover with good vinegar and simmer ¾ of an hour.

Chow Chow.
F. L. A.

1 quart of lima beans, 1 quart of corn, 1 quart of green tomatoes, 1 quart of small pickles, 2 quarts of string beans, 2 heads of cabbage, 3 sweet peppers, 2 strong peppers, celery as much as you prefer, 2 tablespoons of mustard seed, 6 tablespoons of salt, sugar as much as you prefer; boil the beans and corn each separately until soft, then put the rest in boiling vinegar; boil a few moments then mix all together; it is then ready to put in jars; keep air-tight.

Catsup.

1 bushel tomatoes, 12 onions, chopped fine; then strain, boil again, add 3 pints vinegar, boil a while, add 2 pounds sugar, 2 cup salt, 1 large iron spoon allspice, cloves, mace, 2 kinds mus-

tard, 2 of cinnamon, ¼ spoon red pepper, 1½ black; 1 nutmeg, a good ½ pint liquor; mix the spices with some of the catsup; do not add spices until nearly done.

Chow Chow.
Mrs. Ira Rutter.

4 quarts green tomatoes, 2 quarts cut cabbage, 2 quarts cut celery, 2 dozen sliced onions, 1 dozen red sweet peppers, ½ ounce tumeric root, ½ ounce celery seed, ½ ounce whole cloves, ½ ounce black peppers, ½ ounce whole allspice, 2 ounces mustard seed, 1 pound sugar, ½ ounce ground ginger, 2 quarts corn, 1 quart lima beans, ¼ peck string beans, 1 dozen cucumbers. Cook beans till nearly done; salt all 2 hours, then drain, put all in a kettle, cover with vinegar, boil 15 minutes, then bottle.

Chow Chow.

1 large head of cabbage, ¼ peck of green tomatoes, 4 onions, 1 head of cauliflower, 1 bunch of celery, 3 large peppers, 1 red, 1 yellow, and 1 green; ½ dozen cucumbers cut on the cutter and salted over night; do not peel them, merely wash and cut them; cloves and allspice to taste, put in whole. Also celery seed and mustard seed to taste; 1 pound of brown sugar, 3 cents' worth of yellow mustard, the same of cinnamon; cut all on the cutter but the celery, which you will have to use a knife to. Put all on to boil but the cucumbers, cover with good cider vinegar, and boil for 20 minutes, stirring often; when the 20 minutes are up, add the cucumbers and boil a short time until they are soft. This will fill 5 quart jars.

Choice French Pickles.
Mrs. K. H. Mish.

1 head of cabbage, 3 large stalks of celery, 3 onions, slice all fine and salt well; after 24 hours drain well and cover with vinegar, to remain 12 hours, then drain from vinegar, add 4 red peppers and 2 green ones, finely cut up; 1 ounce tumeric, ¼ pound mustard seed, 1 teaspoonful mixed mustard, 1 teaspoonful allspice, ½ spoonful cloves, 1 teaspoonful black pepper, 1 cup olive oil and 1 cup brown sugar; mix well and cover with vinegar.

Chili Sauce.
Mrs. E. W. Herrick, Minneapolis, Minn.

12 large, ripe tomatoes, 4 ripe or 3 green peppers, 2 onions, 2 tablespoons salt, 2 of sugar, 1 of cinnamon; 3 cups of vinegar; peel tomatoes and onions, chop all fine and boil 1½ hours. Bottle and it will keep any length of time. 1 quart of canned tomatoes may be used instead of the ripe ones.

Receipt for Spicing.
Mrs. J. K. Fisher.

To 7 pounds of fruit take 3 pounds of good brown sugar and 1 pint of vinegar. Put the sugar and vinegar on to boil, add 1 teaspoon of cloves, 1 teaspoon of allspice, 2 teaspoons of cinnamon, ½ teaspoon of mace. Put the spices in separate little cheese-cloth bags, and drop into the syrup.

Bordeaux Sauce.
Mrs. Edgar Lamoreaux.

2 gallons chopped cabbage, 1 gallon green tomatoes, sliced; 12 onions, sliced; 1 ounce of whole allspice, 1 ounce of cloves, 1 ounce of ground ginger, ½ pound white mustard seed, ¾ gill salt, 1¾ pounds sugar, 1 gallon vinegar. Boil all together ½ an hour.

Tomato Catsup.
Emma Richards.

½ bushel tomatoes, ½ pint salt, ½ pint vinegar, 2 nutmegs, 3 teaspoons of red pepper, 1 teaspoon of black pepper, 2 teaspoons of cloves, 2 teaspoons of allspice, 2 teaspoons of cinnamon, 1 cup sugar.

French Pickles.
Mrs. Krum.

1 head cabbage, ½ peck green tomatoes, 3 large stalks celery, 12 onions; chop all fine, salt it 24 hours, then drain well with your hand; cover with vinegar for 12 hours, then drain it out of the vinegar and add 4 red and 2 green peppers, then chop fine and mix 1 ounce of yellow turmeric, ¼ pound mustard seed, 1 teaspoon of mixed mustard, 1 teaspoon of pepper, ½ teaspoon of cloves, 1 pound brown sugar, and sweeten to taste, then cover with vinegar.

Green Tomato Sauce, or Pickled Lilly.
Mrs. W. H. Newhard, Allentown.

½ peck green, hard tomatoes, ½ dozen onions, sliced and resliced (crosswise); put a good handful of salt over them, then cover with a plate and put on a press; let stand over night and drain all that green water off; then put into your lined kettle with 1 ounce yellow mustard, about 3 hot peppers, a few cloves if you like, and cidar vinegar enough to cover; do not let them get hot enough to burn; shake them around now and then and after they begin to simmer leave them cook in that way a ½ hour or so. It will take longer if you do not have the tomatoes and onions in pretty small pieces. Celery seed may be put in if desired.

Chilli Sauce.
Mrs. Edgar Lamoreaux.

1 peck ripe tomatoes, 1 cup sugar, 3 tablespoonfuls salt, 8 onions, 4 green peppers, 1 tablespoonful cloves, 1 tablespoonful cinnamon, 1 tablespoonful allspice, 1 quart good cider vinegar; chop peppers and onions fine. Boil 2 hours.

Oil Pickle.
Mrs. K. H. Mish.

100 small cucumbers, 1 quart onions, 2 quarts vinegar, 1 pint olive oil, 1 teaspoon black pepper, 1 ounce celery seed, ¼ pound ground mustard, ¼ pound whole mustard. Pare and slice thin onions and cucumbers, lay in alternate layers, sprinkling with salt; put a heavy weight on top and let stand over night, then drain. Put a teaspoonful of powdered alum in sufficient vinegar (cold) to cover pickles, stir until dissolved, pour over and let stand 4 or 8 hours. Put cucumbers and onions in a glass or stone jar, mix spices with oil, then add gradually the 2 quarts of vinegar and pour over the pickle.

Mustard Pickles.
Mrs. Southan.

50 nice pickles put in hot salt-water over night. Dry and cut up in 1 pint vinegar; boil well; mix ½ pound mustard with vinegar; 1 pound brown sugar. Mix all into smooth batter and boil, being careful not to burn.

Spiced Tomatoes.
Mrs. Robt. Hean.

To spice tomatoes, ripe tomatoes, take vinegar sufficient quantity for the amount of tomatoes to cover, put them in glass jars, then pour the cold vinegar in to see how much it takes; then to every pint of vinegar ½ pound sugar or as much as to sweeten it enough ,and spice to taste. Boil the vinegar, sugar and spices well and let stand and cool off a little, then pour in the jars, close and let stand until next day; then warm again, pour on and close for good.

Spiced Tomato Pickle.
Mrs. J. K. Fisher.

Slice 1 peck of green tomatoes, 4 onions, 4 peppers (red): after all are sliced together then salt well, let stand over night; next morning pour water on and rinse off salt; leave it drain, then put in kettle, add as much vinegar as will cover it; add 1 cup dark sugar, 1 tablespoon of mustard seed, 1 tablespoon of whole allspice, 1 tablespoon of whole cloves, 1 tablespoon of cinnamon, and a few slices of horse radish; boil together till soft, then place in jars. Will keep all winter.

Pickled Cabbage.
Mrs. J. Giles.

Cut the cabbage very fine, and for a 6 gallon jar take a pint cup nearly full of salt, the same amount of horse radish (cut up in small pieces) and 2 heaping tablespoons of white mustard seed. Sprinkle a little salt in the bottom of the jar, then put in a layer of cabbage, and with a potato masher pound the cabbage firmly; then sprinkle on some salt, radish and mustard seed; then put in another layer of cabbage and do as before. Be sure to give every layer of cabbage a thorough pounding. When your jar is full put an inverted plate on the cabbage, and on that put a 20 pound weight. Let it stand until next morning, then drain off the brine that has formed and pour over the cabbage cider vinegar, boiling hot. It spoils vinegar to heat it in iron; use a porcelain kettle or a stone milk crock. Leave the plate on the cabbage to keep from floating, for it must be kept under the vinegar. Tie several thicknesses of cloth over top of jar, then cover closely and set in cool place—some place just above the freezing point.

Chilli Sauce.
Mrs. W. Klopp.

12 large tomatoes, 4 ripe peppers, 3 green peppers, 2 onions, 2 tablespoonfuls of salt, 2 tablespoonfuls of sugar, 1 tablespoonful cinnamon, 3 cups of vinegar. Peel tomatoes and onions and chop separately very fine; add the peppers, chopped, with the other ingredients and boil 1½ hours, and then bottle it.

Dubrex Sauce.
R. M. Brown.

1 gallon green tomatoes, 2 gallons cabbage, cut coarsely; ½ pound white mustard seed, 1 pound brown sugar, 1 gill salt, 1 ounce turmeric, 1 ounce whole allspice, 1 ounce whole cloves, ½ ounce black pepper, 1 dozen onions, 1 ounce celery seed, 1 gallon vinegar; mix together and boil 15 or 20 minutes.

Bordeaux Sauce.
Mrs. J. K. Fisher.

1½ gallons of cut cabbage, ½ gallon of green tomatoes, ½ dozen of onions, 3 peppers, 6 stalks of celery, 1 quart of corn, 1 pint lima beans; the cabbage, tomatoes, onions, peppers, celery all to be cut in small pieces; add ½ ounce turmeric, ½ ounce yellow mustard, ½ ounce brown mustard, ½ ounce black pepper, ½ pound of dark sugar, 3 quarts of vinegar. Boil all together 20 minutes, and fill jars.

Peach Mangoes.
Mrs. Chas. Frantz.

Rub fur off of peach, open at the side and take out the stone, fill with grated horse radish and black mustard seed; take 3 pounds of soft white sugar to 1 quart of vinegar; boil together 3 times and pour over peaches, hot every time; tie the peaches after they are filled, before pouring the syrup over them.

Spiced Grapes.
Mrs. K. H. Mish.

7 pounds grapes, 4 pounds sugar, coffee cup of vinegar, small handful whole cloves.

Mustard Pickles.
Mrs. Edgar Lamoreaux.

1 peck tomatoes, green; ½ peck onions, 3 or 4 cauliflower; boil until tender, slice, cover with salt, let drain over night; add ½ box of mustard, 2 or 3 red peppers; cover with vinegar, and let simmer all day.

Grape Catsup.
Mrs. James Watson.

Cook soft and press through a sieve 5 pounds of ripe grapes, after which stir into the pulp 2½ pounds sugar, 1 pint vinegar, 1 teaspoonful of salt and 1 tablespoonful each of cinnamon, cloves, allspice, and cayenne pepper. Boil down until the catsup is of the proper consistency.

Ripe Tomato Pickles.
Mrs. Lewis Brown.

Pare ripe, sound tomatoes (do not scald); put in a jar; scald spices (tied in a bag) in vinegar and pour while hot over them. This recipe is best for persons who prefer raw tomatoes.

Bordeaux Sauce.
Mrs. D. S. Herr, Pleasant Grove.

2 gallons chopped cabbage, 1 gallon green tomatoes (sliced), 1 dozen onions (cut fine), 1 ounce turmeric, 1 ounce whole cloves, ½ ounce whole allspice, 1 ounce ground ginger, ½ pound white mustard seed, 1½ pounds white sugar, 1¾ gills salt, 1 gallon vinegar. Boil ½ hour.

Chow Chow.
Mrs. J. K. Fisher.

½ peck green tomatoes, 1 small head of cabbage, ½ dozen of red and yellow peppers, ½ dozen of onions, 3 heads of celery; chop these fine the evening before making, each separately. Mix all well with a large handful of salt, except celery; put a cloth in a basket, then place the mixture in and press heavily all night. In the morning add 1 cup of dark sugar, 2 tablespoons yellow mustard, 1 tablespoon black mustard, 1 tablespoon each of cinnamon, cloves, and 1 scant tablespoonful of allspice, 1 cup of grated horse radish, and add the chopped celery; cover with vinegar; boil until tender, place in jars and make air-tight.

Pickled Grapes.

Mrs. C. T. Carson.

Fill a jar with alternate layers of sugar and bunches of nice grapes, just ripe; fill 1-3 full of good, cold vinegar and cover tightly.

Grape Catsup.

Take 5 pounds of grapes, boiled to a pulp and sifted; add 2 pounds of sugar, 1 pint of vinegar, 1 tablespoon each of cinnamon, cloves, allspice, and 1 teaspoonful of pepper. Boil 2 hours and put up in glass jars.

Cold Catsup.

Katharine Behney.

½ peck ripe tomatoes, cut with knife; 2 pints of vinegar, 3 green and 3 red peppers, ½ cup mustard seed (yellow), 2 tablespoons of black pepper, salt to taste, 1 large stalk of celery, 1 onion, chopped, and mix all well. Bottle air-tight.

Chow Chow.

1 peck green tomatoes, 1 quart cabbage, 1½ pounds sugar, ½ pound mustard, 1 ounce celery seed, 1 ounce cloves ½ ounce allspice, ½ ounce pepper, 1 quart vinegar.

Tomato Chow Chow.

M. A. McFarland.

6 large, ripe tomatoes, 1 onion, 1 green pepper, 1 tablespoon of salt, 2 tablespoons of brown sugar, 2 cups vinegar. Stew gently 1 hour.

Chow Chow.

Mrs. W. H. Goodyear.

½ peck tomatoes, 1 onion, ½ cup salt, ½ ounce yellow mustard, 3 sweet peppers, hot peppers to taste, 1 ounce of cloves, 1 tablespoon allspice, 1 stalk celery, ½ cup sugar.

Chow Chow.

Mrs. C. M. Light.

2 quarts green tomatoes, chopped; 2 quarts cabbage, chopped; 4 onions; salt and drain; 3 large peppers, 2 heads of celery, ½ cup of sugar, 2 tablespoons mustard seed, 1 of celery seed, 1 of black pepper. Cover with vinegar, heat thoroughly and seal.

PICKLES.

Chow Chow.
M. A. McFarland.

1 quart large cucumbers, cut lengthwise; 1 quart small ones, whole; 1 quart onions, 1 large cauliflower, 1 quart green tomatoes; put cucumbers in brine and scald the rest in salt and water; add some peppers and other spices if desired; to 2 quarts vinegar add $1\frac{1}{2}$ cups sugar, 1 cup flour, 6 tablespoons mustard; scald the vinegar, flour and mustard, and pour over pickles. Put up in bottles.

Chow Chow.
Mary Richards.

5-8 peck of green tomatoes, 2 dozen ears of corn, $\frac{1}{4}$ peck of onions, 2 dozen medium sized cucumbers, 2 bunches celery, 1 large head of cabbage, 1 dozen sweet peppers, 10 cents' worth mustard; cover with vinegar. Cut up everything but the corn and celery, sprinkle with salt and let stand over night. Drain next morning and boil all together from 5 to 10 minutes; the vinegar must not be added till morning.

Chow Chow.
Mrs. M. H. Parker.

$\frac{1}{2}$ peck green tomatoes, 2 large heads of cabbage, 15 onions, 25 cucumbers, 1 pint grated horse-radish, $\frac{1}{2}$ pound mixed mustard seed, 1 ounce celery seed, $\frac{1}{4}$ cup of ground black pepper, $\frac{1}{4}$ cup turmeric; cut tomatoes, onions, cabbage and cucumbers in small pieces, pack in salt over night; drain, then put in vinegar and water for a day or two, drain again; boil spices with $\frac{1}{2}$ gallon of vinegar and 3 pounds brown sugar, pour over pickle while hot; repeat this for 3 mornings; then mix 5 ounces of dry mustard with $\frac{1}{2}$ pint of salad oil and 2 quarts more of vinegar and pour over the pickle when cold.

Chow Chow.
Mrs. K. H. Mish.

$\frac{1}{4}$ peck green tomatoes, $\frac{1}{4}$ peck onions, 5 dozen cucumbers; slice fine, putting in a few small whole ones; 1 pint of red and green peppers, chopped fine; add a pint of salt; let stand over night; drain well and add 1 ounce mace, 1 ounce white mustard seed, 1 ounce celery seed, 1 ounce turmeric, 1 ounce whole cloves, 3 tablespoonfuls of yellow mustard seed, ½ pound brown sugar, root of grated horse-radish, 1 gallon of fine sour vinegar. Boil 30 minutes.

Spiced Fruit.

7 pounds of fruit, 3 pounds sugar, 1 pint vinegar, 5 cents' worth cloves and 5 cents' worth cinnamon.

Chilli Sauce.
Tillie Follweiler.

12 tomatoes (large), 2 onions, 1 mango, 1 cup vinegar, 1 even tablespoon salt, 1 tablespoonful sugar, cinnamon and cloves 1 teaspoon of each. Peel and boil tomatoes as for stewing, chop onions and mango fine and add; boil an hour, pour in bottles and seal.

Cold Catsup.

½ peck of tomatoes, 1 bunch of celery, 2 green peppers, ½ cup of black mustard, ½ cup of yellow mustard, 1 red pepper, ½ cup salt, 1 quart cider vinegar.

Catsup.

½ bushel ripe tomatoes, cut up and boil and rub through sieve; ½ teacup vinegar, 1 cup sugar, 3 tablespoonfuls salt, 1 tablespoonful ground cinnamon, 1 tablespoonful allspice, 1 tablespoonful cloves.

Catsup.

To 3 quarts of tomato juice, ½ pint of vinegar, 2 cents' worth of cinnamon, 2 cents' worth of cloves, 2 cents' worth of salt, ½ cup sugar, 1 teaspoonful pepper, 1 onion. Put the spices in when almost done; mix them with a little vinegar first.

Chilli Sauce.
F. L. A.

1 basket of ripe tomatoes, 9 red peppers, 6 onions, 8 cups of vinegar, 9 heaping teaspoons of salt, 18 large spoons of sugar, 9 teaspoons of cloves, 9 of allspice and 9 of ginger; chop peppers and onions fine, boil with tomatoes 1 hour, then strain through a fine sieve, after strained put back on the stove, add the rest of the ingredients and boil until thick.

Pepper Cabbage.
Mrs. James Scott.

1 head of cabbage, cut as for slaw; ½ dozen peppers, cut fine; salt, mustard seed, and celery seed to taste; mix thoroughly and cover with vinegar.

Chilli Sauce.
Mrs. J. H. Roberts.

24 large tomatoes, 6 onions, 5 small peppers, 2 cups vinegar, 4 tablespoons brown sugar, 2 tablespoons salt, celery seed and mustard seed.

Prepared Mustard.

Take 3 teaspoons ground mustard, 1 of flour (2 if the mustard seems very strong), ½ teaspoon sugar; pour boiling water on these and mix into a thick paste; when cold add vinegar enough to make it ready for use, and serve with salt.

Chilli Sauce.
Mrs. Robert Wagner.

12 large tomatoes, 1 large onion, 4 red peppers, chop all together fine; 2 cups sugar, 1 tablespoon of salt, 1 of vinegar, 1 teaspoon each of allspice and cloves. Boil until quite thick, then bottle and seal.

Catsup.
Mrs. J. W. Harbeson.

½ bushel tomatoes, 1 pound sugar, 1 pint vinegar, 2 tablespoons cinnamon, 1 tablespoon cloves, 1 tablespoon of allspice, 1 tablespoon of mustard, 1 teaspoon of salt, 1 teaspoon black pepper, cayenne pepper to suite taste.

Pickles.
Mrs. F.

To 1 quart jar of cucumbers add 8 or 10 small onions, 4 to 5 bay leaves, 2 to 4 grape leaves, heaping teaspoon of salt, 1 tablespoon of whole allspice, 2 or 3 small peppers, 1 tablespoonful of yellow mustard seed; fill the jars, bring vinegar to a boiling point, pour over and close.

Jersey Peaches.

7 pounds fruit scalded, 3 pounds sugar, 1 pint of vinegar.

PICKLES.

Sweet Pickles.

Make a brine that will bear an egg, and put the pickles in for 2 days; then pour the brine off, boil and pour over the pickles 2 days in succession; then take equal portions of vinegar and water, boil and pour over 2 days in succession; this will make 6 days. The seventh day take 1 quart of vinegar, ¼ cup of whole black pepper, ¼ cup of whole allspice, ¼ cup of whole cloves, ¼ cup of green ginger, cut in small pieces; 1 cup of mustard seed, 1 cup of horse-radish, cut into small pieces, 1 pound sugar; let all come to a boil and pour over the pickles boiling hot; you can put them in jars or leave all in one large jar; will keep just as well. You can judge from the quantity of brine what quantity of vinegar to use.

In looking through this book....

Stop, Read

about our

Shoes.

As they are made for wear and tare. Our prices are as low as the lowest. We guarantee fit and satisfaction. We are in a position to do the finest kind of repairing. Give us a call and let us prove what we say.

New York Shoe Store,
W. F. Garrett, 125 N. 8th St., Lebanon, Pa.

PRESERVES, JELLIES, ETC.

"Sweet to the sweet."—Shakespeare.

Plum Preserves.
Mrs. I. H. Shearer.

Allow equal weights sugar and plums, add sufficient water to the sugar to make a thick syrup; boil, skim and pour over the plums (previously washed, picked and placed in a stone jar) and cover with a plate. The next day drain off syrup, boil, skim and pour over plums. Repeat this for 3 or 4 days. Place plums and syrup in the preserving kettle and boil very slowly for $\frac{1}{2}$ an hour. Put in stone jars, cover with papers, like jellies, or seal in cans.

Lemon Butter.
Mrs. H. K. Aurand, Tamaqua.

$\frac{1}{4}$ pound butter, 1 pound pulverized sugar, yolks of 6 eggs, well beaten; whites of 4 eggs, well beaten; juice of 3 lemons, grated rind of only 2. Melt butter and rub with sugar to a cream; mix whites and yolks with juice and rind to a smooth paste; then mix the whole; put into a double boiler, and boil 20 minutes, stirring well.

Quince Marmalade.
Mrs. E. U. Sowers.

1 tincup of grated quince, 4 tincups of water, 4 pounds of sugar.

Lemon Butter.

2 lemons (rind and juice), 2 cups sugar, 1 small lump butter, 2 tablespoons of cornstarch, 2 cups water, 1 or 2 eggs. Thoroughly mix lemons and sugar in a pan; add the butter and put on the stove to melt; while melting, mix cornstarch and water, and stir into the lemons. Let it boil for 15 minutes, stirring it to prevent burning, and when nearly done, add the eggs, which have been previously well beaten.

Pineapple Marmalade.
Mrs. E. U. Sowers.

1 pint of grated pineapple, 1 pint of water, 2 pints of sugar.

Lemon Honey.
Louisa C. Light.

1 grated lemon (rind and juice), 1½ cups of sugar, ½ cup of butter, 1 cup of water, 2 tablespoonfuls of cornstarch. Cook till thick, stirring while cooking. Nice as a sauce, or to put between layer cake.

Lemon Butter.
F. L. A.

Small cup and a half of white sugar, 3 eggs, 1 lemon, piece of butter the size of a small walnut. Beat the eggs; then put in the sugar, lemon and butter. Boil till thick, stirring occasionally. Takes the place of preserves or jelly.

Lemon Jelly.

½ pack gelatine, ½ cup cold water, 1 pint boiling water, 1 cup sugar, 2-3 cup lemon juice. Soak gelatine 1 hour in cold water; add boiling water, sugar and lemon juice. Strain through napkin into moulds which have been wet in cold water.

Apple Butter.

Take 1½ pecks of sour apples to 5 pounds common sugar. Boil from 3 to 4 hours. By adding a little old apple butter it will make it better. First boil the apples soft, then mash them through a colander; then put them over to boil as above stated.

Canned Pineapple.
C. W. Cyphers, Minneapolis, Minn.

Peel and slice; make syrup in proportion of 2½ pounds of best white granulated sugar to nearly 3 pints of water; boil 5 minutes; skim or strain; add fruit, and let it boil. Have cans hot; fill, and seal up as soon as possible.

Pineapple Preserves.
Mrs. J. C. Urich, Marquette, Mich.

To 1 grated pineapple take 3 pounds sugar and 1 pint water. Boil pineapple soft; then add sugar. Do not stir.

Pineapple Jelly.

Soak ½ box gelatine 1 hour in cup cold water; stir in cup sugar; add ½ cup liquor drained from a can of pineapple, ½ pint boiling water; strain; stir in cupful fruit, chopped fine. Turn into mould and set on ice.

Cranberry Jelly.
C. G. Crane, Caldwell, N. J.

Place fruit in kettle, with water enough to keep from burning; let remain on the fire until thoroughly scalded; add 1 pound sugar to every pint; boil and skim; test by dropping a little into cold water (when it does not mingle with the water it is done); rinse glasses in cold water before pouring in the jelly, to prevent sticking. The pulp may be melted and used for sauce.

Cranberry Jelly.
Mrs. R. S. Malsberger.

Put 1 quart of cranberries, which have been carefully picked and washed, to boil in 1 pint of cold water; have ready in a bowl 1 pint of white sugar; when the cranberries are perfectly soft, mash them, while hot, through a very fine colander into the bowl which contains the sugar, and stir until the sugar is dissolved; then pour into moulds. If the cranberries are good and no more water added, this way of cooking them makes beautiful moulds for the table.

Quince Honey.

4 quinces to 1 quart water, 3 pounds sugar. The quinces must be grated, and boil until stiff enough.

Quince Honey.
H. M. M.

1 large quince, 1 pound of soft A sugar, 1 pint of water. Boil 20 minutes.

Canning Fruit.
Mrs. John T. Atkins.

To 6 jars of fruit, 2 pounds of sugar, 3 quarts of water. Let the sugar and water come to a boil, then stand away to get cold. Fill the jars with fruit, pour the syrup over them, cover lightly with the lid, and stand in a kettle of cold water. Let this water come to a boil, then lift out the jars and seal them.

Cleveland's Baking Powder

Manufactured originally by Cleveland Brothers, Albany, N. Y., now by the Cleveland Baking Powder Company, New York.

has been used by American housewives for twenty-five years, and those who have used it longest praise it most.

It is perfectly pure and wholesome.

Its composition is stated on every can.

It is always uniform and reliable.

It does the most work and the best work.

It is the strongest of all pure cream of tartar powders, as shown by the U. S. and Canadian Government Reports.

All the leading teachers of cookery and writers on domestic science use and recommend it, as :—

Mrs. Sarah T. Rorer,
  Prin. Philadelphia Cooking School.
Mrs. Emma P. Ewing,
  Principal Chautauqua School of Cookery.
Mrs. Carrie M. Dearborn,
  Late Prin. Boston Cooking School.
Mrs. D. A. Lincoln,
  Author of "Boston Cook Book."
Miss Fannie M. Farmer,
  Principal Boston Cooking School.
Miss C. C. Bedford,
  Supt. New York Cooking School.
Marion Harland,
  Author of "Common Sense in the Household."
Mrs. Eliza R. Parker,
  "Author of Economical Housekeeping."
Miss Kate E. Whitaker, Supt. of Cookery in Public Schools, San Franciso, Cal.

Our book of 400 choice receipts mailed free. Send stamp and address. Cleveland Baking Powder Co., 81 & 83 Fulton Street, New York.

CAKES.

Aye, to the leavening, but here's yet in the word hereafter the kneading, the making of the cake, the heating of the oven, and the baking. Nay, you must stay the cooling, too, or you may chance to burn your mouth.—Shakespeare.

Cake-making Tips.

Successful cake making depends on about 20 things:

Proper materials.

A correct recipe.

Following directions explicitly.

Accurate weights and measurements.

Compounding the ingredients in their proper order.

Having everything in readiness before commencing to mix the ingredients.

Having all the ingredients at the right temperature.

Not suspending the mixing until the cake is ready for the oven.

Beating much or little, according to the kind of cake, and always in one direction.

Whipping the whites of the eggs to a coarse, moderately stiff froth rather than a fine, stiff one.

Sifting the baking powder and flour together 2 or 3 times.

Folding the flour in carefully instead of by strong circular strokes.

Placing in the oven as soon as the baking powder is added.

Greasing the tin with sweet lard rather than butter, and sifting a little dry flour over.

Opening and shutting the oven door very gently during the process of baking.

Not turning while in the oven if it can be avoided.

Keeping fruit over night in a warm room; dredging it thoroughly with flour, and stirring it in lightly the last thing.

Making the paper or paste lining of a tin for fruit cake or a large loaf-cake an inch higher at the sides, to support a paper cover and prevent its baking too hard.

Lining tins for loaf-cake with oiled paper.

In baking loaf-cake remember that unless you place a piece of paper over for protection at first, a top crust will be formed at once that prevents rising. When cake is well raised remove paper for browning on top.

1, 2, 3, 4 Cake.
Vivian Hummel.

2-3 of a cup of shortening, 2 cups of sugar, 3 cups of flour, 4 eggs, 1 cup of milk; beat the shortening to a cream, adding the sugar gradually, beating all the while. Beat the eggs very lightly and add them to the shortening and sugar; add the flour and whatever flavoring extract you may prefer, about ½ teaspoonful. Bake in a moderate oven.

Mountain Ash Cake.

1 pound of sugar, ¾ of a cup of butter, 6 eggs, beaten separately; 1 cup of thick milk or sweet milk and 2 spoonfuls of Cleveland baking powder, 1 teaspoonful of soda, 3 cups of flour. Bake in layers.

Mountain Cake.
Mrs. S. B. Cox.

1 cup of sugar, ½ cup of butter, ½ cup of sweet milk, ½ cup of corn starch, 1 cup of flour, whites of 6 eggs, a little vanilla, 2 teaspoonfuls Cleveland baking powder. Bake in layers.

Frosting for above.—Whites of 5 eggs, 20 tablespoonfuls of sifted sugar, beaten very light, and a little vanilla. Spread between layers and on the outside of the cake.

White Mountain Cake.

3 cups sugar, 1 cup butter, 5 eggs, 1 cup thick milk, 5 cups flour, 2 teaspoons cream of tartar, teaspoon baking soda.

Icing for above cake.—1 pound pulverized sugar, 1 cocoanut, the whites of 4 eggs; sprinkle cocoanut on cake after it has been iced.

Ribbon Cake.
Mrs. John H. Diehl.

1 cup sugar, ¼ cup butter, ½ cup sweet milk, 1½ cups flour, 1½ teaspoons Cleveland baking powder, whites of 4 eggs, 1

Cottolene requires only 2-3 the quantity of lard. Use it.

teaspoon vanilla; take ½ of batter for white layers and balance for pink layers. For the other layers take 1 cup sugar, ¼ cup butter, ½ cup sweet milk, 1¼ cups flour, yolks of 4 eggs, 2 teaspoons Cleveland baking powder; use ½ for yellow layers, the other ½ mixed with chocolate.

Ice Cream Cake.
Mrs. J. Dewald.

2 cups sugar, 1 cup of sweet milk, 1 cup of butter, 2 cups of flour, 1 cup of corn starch, whites of 8 eggs, 2 teaspoons of cream of tartar, 1 teaspoon of soda, 2 teaspoons of vanilla; bake in jelly tins.

Filling.—Whites of 4 eggs, 4 cups of granulated sugar, ½ pint of water, 2 teaspoons citric acid, 2 teaspoons vanilla; pour boiling water on sugar; boil until clear and will candy in water. Pour the boiling syrup over the eggs, well beaten, and beat until cold and stiff cream; before quite cold add the citric acid and vanilla. Place about 1 inch thick between the layers of cake.

Molasses Cake.

1 cup of molasses, ½ cup of brown sugar, ½ cup of butter and lard, mixed, 1 cup of water, 1 egg, 1 teaspoon of soda; add flour to stiffen.

Sunshine Cake.
Mrs. R. H. Graeff.

Whites of 7 small, fresh eggs; yolks of 5, 1 cup granulated sugar, 2-3 cup flour, 1-3 teaspoon cream of tartar, and a pinch of salt. Sift, measure and set aside flour and sugar as for Angel cake. Beat yolks of eggs thoroughly, then after washing beater, beat whites about half, add cream of tartar and beat until very, very stiff; stir in sugar lightly, then beaten yolks thoroughly, then add flour; put in tube pan and in the oven at once. Will bake in 35 to 50 minutes.

Ribbon Cake.
Mrs. Peter Aurand, Tamaqua.

2 cups of white sugar, 1 cup butter, 1 cup water, 3 cups flour, 4 eggs, 2 heaping teaspoonfuls Cleveland baking powder. Take 1-3 of batter, add to it 1 cup of raisins (stoned), 1

Cottolene requires only 2-3 the quantity of lard. Use it.

cup of currants, 1 teaspoonful cloves, 1 teaspoonful cinnamon, ½ a nutmeg. This will make 3 good sized layers. The one containing the fruit to be placed in the middle; ice with boiled icing.

Ice Cream Cake.
Mrs. H. Graeff.

2 cups of sugar, 1 cup of butter, 1 cup of milk, ½ cup of corn starch, 2½ cups of flour, whites of 5 eggs, 2 teaspoonfuls of Cleveland baking powder. Cream butter and sugar, add milk and corn starch, then flour with the baking powder sifted in, and then the whites of eggs, well beaten; flavor with vanilla. Bake in 3 layers. Ice with the whites of 3 eggs and pulverized sugar flavored with vanilla.

Molasses Plum Cake.

3 eggs, 1 cup of brown sugar, 1 cup of molasses, 1 cup of sour milk, 1 piece of butter, size of an egg; 1 piece of lard, size of an egg; 1 pound of currants, ½ pound of raisins, 1 teaspoonful of cloves, 1 teaspoonful of soda.

Ice Cream Cake.
Mrs. R. H. Graeff.

½ cup butter, 2 cups sugar, 1 cup milk, 3 cups flour, 3 eggs, all the yolk and the white of 1 egg, 1½ teaspoonfuls Cleveland baking powder, 1 teaspoonful lemon extract. This will make 3 cakes.

Icing for the same.—2 cups white sugar in a small ½ cup of boiling water; boil 10 minutes; keep stirring while it boils; beat the whites of 2 eggs very light; pour in while boiling; then stir till cold and stiff; add 1 teaspoonful lemon extract; put this between the cakes; a little more sugar for the top if

Dolly Warden Cake.

2 cups sugar, ½ cup butter, 1 cup sweet milk, 4 eggs, 2 teaspoonfuls Cleveland baking powder. Beat well together, put ½ the quantity in another dish; add to this 1 cup raisins, stoned and chopped; ½ cup currants, ½ nutmeg, 2 teaspoonfuls cinnamon, 2 teaspoonfuls cloves. Bake in jelly tins and put icing between.

Cottolene requires only 2-3 the quantity of lard. Use it.

Ice Cream Cake.
Mrs. W. Klopp.

½ cup butter, 1½ cupfuls pulverized sugar, 2 cups of flour, ½ cup of milk, whites of 5 eggs, 2 level teaspoonfuls of Cleveland baking powder, ½ teaspoonful of vanilla; beat the butter to cream and gradually beat into it the sugar and then the vanilla. Now add the milk and also the whites of the eggs, beaten to a stiff froth. Finally stir in the flour and baking powder mixed together. Pour this batter into shallow cake pans and having been well battered, bake in a moderate oven for 20 or 30 minutes; when cold, ice.

Sunshine Sponge Cake.

Whites of 7 eggs, yolks of 5, 1 cup fine granulated sugar, 1 scant cup flour, measured after sifting 5 times; ¼ teaspoonful cream of tartar, 1 teaspoonful orange extract. Beat yolks till thick and set aside. Now add a pinch of salt and the cream of tartar to the whites and beat till very stiff; add sugar, beat thoroughly; then add flavoring and beaten yolks and carefully stir in the flour. Bake in moderate oven 40 or 50 minutes. Invert pan to cool when cake is done.

Marble Cake.

½ cup of butter, 1 cup of white sugar, ½ cup of sweet milk, 2 cups of flour, ½ teaspoon soda, ½ teaspoon of cream of tartar, 5 eggs, white.

Dark part.—½ cup of butter, 1 cup of brown sugar, ½ cup of sweet milk, ½ teaspoon soda, 2 teaspoons cream of tartar, 1 teaspoon cloves and allspice, 2 cups of flour, yolks of 5 eggs.

Ice Cream Cake.

Take whites of 8 eggs, beaten light; 2 cups of sugar, 1 cup of butter, 2 cups of flour, 1 cup of corn starch, 1 cup of milk, 2 teaspoonfuls of Cleveland baking powder.

Icing.—Whites of 3 eggs, beaten light; 3 cups granulated sugar, 1-3 of a pint of boiling water; pour over the sugar and boil fast till clear. Pour boiling sugar over eggs and beat till it is stiff cream; add 1 teaspoonful of citric acid; flavor with vanilla.

Cottolene requires only 2-3 the quantity of lard. Use it.

Sponge Cake.
Mrs. D. M. Karmany.

Beat the whites of 5 eggs stiff; add the yolks, one at a time; beat well; add 1¼ cups soft white sugar, put in slowly; beat 10 minutes; flavor; sift in slowly 1 cup flour; flavor with vanilla.

Feather Cake.

Rub ¼ cup butter to a cream; add 1 cup of sugar; beat the yolks of 2 eggs very light and add to the butter and sugar; flavor. Beat the whites stiff and dry, put in last; add ½ cup milk, 1½ cups flour, sifted with 1½ teaspoonfuls of Cleveland baking powder; a pinch of salt. Bake in a moderate oven until the cake shrinks from the pan.

Marble Cake.
Mrs. Moore, Indianapolis, Ind.

Light part.—1½ cups of white sugar, ½ cup of butter, ½ cup of milk, 2 teaspoonfuls of Cleveland baking powder, whites of 5 eggs, 2½ cups of flour, extract of lemon. Dark part.—1 cup of brown sugar, ½ cup of Orleans molasses, ½ cup of butter, ¼ cup sweet milk, 2 teaspoonfuls Cleveland baking powder, 2¼ cups flour, yolks of 5 eggs, 2 tablespoonfuls of cinnamon, 1 tablespoonful of cloves, 1 tablespoonful of allspice, 1 tablespoonful of nutmeg.

Marble Cake.

White part.—1 cup of white sugar, ½ cup of butter, ½ cup of sweet milk, 2 cups of flour, whites of 5 eggs, 1 teaspoon soda, 1 teaspoon of cream of tartar. Brown part.—1 cup of brown sugar, 1 cup of butter, ½ cup of sweet milk, 2 cups of flour, yolks of 5 eggs, 1 tablespoon cinnamon, ½ tablespoon of cloves, ½ teaspoon cream of tartar. Drop the light and dark into the pan alternately.

Sponge Cake.
Mrs. Pilcher, Jackson, Mo.

6 eggs, 2 teacups pulverized sugar; beat yolks and sugar to a cream; add 1½ cups of flour with 2 small teaspoons Cleveland baking powder in it; then add the whites, beaten to a stiff froth, and stir all slowly till top is covered with bubbles. Bake in moderately quick oven.

Cottolene requires only 2-3 the quantity of lard. Use it.

Sallie's Cake.

Yolks of 2 eggs, 1¼ cups granulated sugar, ¼ cup butter, 1 cup milk, 2½ cups flour, 3 teaspoons Cleveland baking powder. Cream yolks, butter and sugar together, add milk and flour, stirring thoroughly; flavor to taste. Bake in 3 square layer pans; ice thickly in the pans with the 2 whites of eggs after cake is cold, cutting it out in squares when ready to serve.

Ice Cream Cake.
Miss Killian.

2 cups granulated sugar, 1 cup of butter, 1 cup sweet milk, 2½ cups flour, ½ cup corn starch, whites of 8 eggs, 1 teaspoon soda, 2 teaspoons cream of tartar, 1 teaspoon of vanilla; work sugar and butter to a cream.

Sponge Cake.
Mrs. S. S. Boltz.

5 eggs, ½ pint sugar, ½ pint flour, 2 teaspoons Cleveland baking powder; beat yolks and sugar well; then add flour and baking powder; last add whites of eggs, well beaten.

Water Sponge Cake.
Mrs. S. E. Breslin.

7 eggs, 3 cups white sugar, 3 cups flour, 3 teaspoons Cleveland baking powder, 1 cup hot water; beat the whites alone; beat the yolks and sugar together, adding cup at a time; then stir flour and baking powder in slowly; then add whites of eggs; lastly cup of hot water.

Leopard Cake.
Mrs. Amelia Ohlwiler, Altoona.

White.—Whites of 8 eggs, 2 cups of sugar, 2½ cups of flour, ½ cup of butter, ½ cup of sour cream, ½ teaspoon of soda, 1½ teaspoons of cream of tartar.

Gold.—Yolks of 8 eggs, 1½ cups of sugar, 2 cups of flour, ½ cup of butter, ½ cup of sour cream, ½ teaspoon of soda, 1 teaspoon of cream of tartar.

Drop alternately a spoon of the white and yellow dough in 2-pound cake dishes.

Cottolene requires only 2-3 the quantity of lard. Use it.

Leopard Cake.

2 cups sugar, ½ cup butter, yolks of 2 eggs; beat this well; add ½ cup sweet milk, ½ cup cold water, 2½ cups flour, with 3 teaspoonfuls of Cleveland baking powder mixed in it; beat the whites to a stiff froth; add last. After the dough is all mixed, take out a cupful, and mix in with it nutmeg, cinnamon and cloves to taste. Line tins with greased paper; put in batter; then drop the spiced part on in spots.

Marble Cake.
Mrs. J. D. Keefer, Columbia.

White Part.—½ cup of butter, 1½ cups sugar, ½ cup of sweet milk, 2 cups flour, whites of 4 eggs, 2 teaspoonfuls of Cleveland baking powder.

Dark Part.—½ cup butter, 1 cup brown sugar, ½ cup of molasses, ½ cup of sweet milk, yolks of 4 eggs, 2 cups flour, cinnamon, nutmeg and cloves, 2 teaspoonfuls of Cleveland baking powder.

Mountain Ash Cake.
Mary Stover.

1 pound sugar, 1 cup of butter, 1 cup of sweet milk, 3 cups of flour, the whites of 10 eggs, 2 teaspoons of Cleveland baking powder.

Fence-rail Cake.

1 pound of sugar, 5 eggs, 1 cup of thick milk, 1 teaspoon of soda, 1 of cream of tartar, 1 nutmeg.

Cream Sponge Cake.
Mary Stover.

1 pound sugar, 1 cup butter, 1 cup sweet milk, 2 cups flour, 1 cup corn starch, yolks of 10 eggs, 3 teaspoons of Cleveland baking powder.

Banana Cake.

2 cups sugar, 4 eggs, 1 cup sweet milk, 2 teaspoons Cleveland baking powder, 1 cup butter and lard mixed, 3 cups flour.

Icing.—White of 1 egg, beaten light; add 6 tablespoons pulverized sugar; cut banana in thin slices; ice each layer and place the bananas on each layer, leaving bananas off the top layer.

Cottolene requires only 2-3 the quantity of lard. Use it.

White Mountain Cake.
Mrs. Kohr.

1 pound butter, 1½ pounds sugar, 2½ pounds flour, 10 eggs, 1½ teaspoons soda, ½ pint cream.

Irish Rag Cake.
Mrs. J. H. Roberts.

3 cups of sugar, 1 cup of butter, 1 cup of sour cream, 6 eggs, 1 tablespoonful of cream of tartar, 1 teaspoonful of soda, 3 cups of flour.

Cream Sponge Cake.
Mrs. John H. Diehl.

Beat 2 eggs in a cup of sweet cream, 1 cup sugar, a pinch of salt, 1½ cups flour, ½ teaspoon soda, 1 teaspoon cream of tartar; beat thoroughly before putting in pan; flavor with lemon.

Cocoanut Cake.
Mrs. Chas. H. Rockel, Allentown.

1 cup sugar, ½ cup butter, 3 eggs, ½ cup milk, 1 cup flour, ½ cup corn starch, 1 teaspoon Cleveland baking powder.

Rye Cake.

1½ cups sour milk, 1½ cups rye flour, 1 teaspoon soda, 1 tablespoon sugar, pinch salt; bake in gem pans. This makes 1 dozen.

Feather Cake.
Mrs. Chas. H. Rockel, Allentown.

2 cups pulverized sugar, ½ cup butter, 1 cup sweet milk, 2½ cups flour, yolks of 4 eggs, 2½ teaspoons Cleveland baking powder.

Simple Sponge Cake.
H. M. M.

3 eggs, 1 cup of sugar, and 1 cup of flour. Beat the eggs very light; then add the sugar; stir in the flour and 1 teaspoonful of water; flavor to taste.

White Mountain Cake.
Mrs. Geo. Stanley.

2 cups of sugar, ½ cup of butter, 1 cup of sour milk, 2½ cups of flour, 3 eggs, 1 teaspoon of soda, ½ teaspoon of cream of tartar.

Cottolene requires only 2-3 the quantity of lard. Use it.

Butter Sponge Cake.

1 pound sugar, 9 eggs, 1 pint flour, 4 tablespoons melted butter; put butter in last.

Shoo-fly Cake.
Mrs. John Killian.

Put 1 teaspoonful of soda in a teacup; pour full of boiling water; pour this on 1 cup of molasses and stir. For the crumbs take 1 cup of butter, 2 cups of sugar and $4\frac{3}{4}$ cups flour. Bake with crust.

Cocoanut Cake.
Mrs. Ebright.

1 cup of butter, 3 cups of sugar, 4 cups of flour, 1 teaspoonful of soda, 2 of cream of tartar, $\frac{1}{2}$ cocoanut, 5 eggs, 1 cup thick milk; beat whites to a froth.

White Mountain Cake.
Mrs. A. M. Ayers.

2 cups soft white sugar, $\frac{1}{2}$ cup butter, $1\frac{1}{2}$ cups sweet milk, 3 cups flour, 2 teaspoonfuls Cleveland baking powder, the whites of 4 eggs, flavor with lemon. Bake in layers and ice.

Lafayette Cake.

$2\frac{1}{2}$ cups sugar, $\frac{3}{4}$ cup butter; beat to a cream; 4 eggs, beat whites to a froth; 1 tablespoon Cleveland baking powder, 1 cup sweet milk, $3\frac{1}{2}$ cups flour; to use soda take 1 teaspoon of soda, 1 teaspoon cream of tartar.

Rolled Sponge Cake.
Mrs. Henry Cole, Allentown.

3 eggs, 1 cup sugar, 1 cup flour, 1 teaspoon Cleveland baking powder, 6 teaspoons cold water.

Feather Cake.
Mrs. Englehart.

2 cups of sugar, $\frac{1}{2}$ cup of butter, 1 cup of sweet milk, 2 eggs, 3 cups of flour, 3 teaspoons Cleveland baking powder.

Hot Water Sponge Cake.
Mrs. Hopewell.

2 cups sugar, 4 eggs, 2 cups of flour, 2 teaspoons Cleveland baking powder; mix sugar, eggs and flour together, add 1 cup hot water last. Bake in jelly pan.

Cottolene requires only 2-3 the quantity of lard. Use it.

CAKES.

White Mountain Cake.
Hannah Phillips, Northumberland.

1 cup sugar, ½ cup of butter, ½ cup sweet milk, ½ cup of corn. starch, 1 cup of flour, whites of 6 eggs, a little vanilla, 2 teaspoonfuls Cleveland baking powder. Bake in layers.

Frosting for above.—Whites of 5 eggs, 20 tablespoonfuls sifted sugar, beaten very light; a little vanilla. Spread between layers and outside of cake.

Sponge Cake Roll.

2 cups of sugar, 2 cups of flour, 6 eggs, 2 teaspoonfuls of Cleveland baking powder; if batter is too stiff, take another egg. Use jelly for icing.

Feather Cake.
Mrs. Ebright.

3 cups sugar, 1 cup sweet milk, 2 teaspoons Cleveland baking powder, ½ cup butter mixed, 3 cups flour.

Jelly Roll.

Mix thoroughly together while dry, 1 cup flour, 1 teaspoon Cleveland baking powder and sift. Add 1 cup of sugar, 4 eggs and 1 tablespoon of cold water. Bake quickly in long, shallows tins; as soon as it is ready to slip from the pans, spread jelly on the bottom, and roll up, then roll a napkin tight around it until cooled.

Leopard Cake.
Mrs. Krum.

2 cups granulated sugar, 3 eggs, ¾ cup butter, creamed; 1 cup of milk and water, ½ of each; 3 cups flour; take 4 tablespoons of it, cut, mix with spices and drop in between.

Ice Cream Cake.
Tillie Follweiler.

1 pound sugar, 1 cup butter, creamed together; 1 cup sweet milk, whites of 5 eggs, beaten stiff; 2 teaspoons Cleveland baking powder, 3 cups flour.

Icing.—Whites of 2 eggs, 2 cups sugar, 10 tablespoons water; boil sugar and water till it will spin a thread; stir in beaten whites of eggs and beat till cold; flavor with vanilla.

Cottolene requires only 2-3 the quantity of lard. Use it.

CAKES.

Ice Cream Cake.
Miss Bertha Ramsay.

1 cup butter, 2½ cups sugar, 4 cups flour, 1 cup sweet milk, 5 eggs, 2 teaspoons cream of tartar, 1 teaspoon soda; flavor.

Lafayette Cake.
Miss Bertha Ramsay.

2 cups sugar, 1 cup butter, 1 cup sweet milk, 4 cups of flour, 2 eggs, 1 teaspoon soda, 2 teaspoons cream of tartar. Bake in 3 layers; flavor.

Water Sponge Cake.
Mrs. Crowther.

4 eggs, 2 cups sugar, 3 cups flour, ½ cup water, 2 teaspoons yeast powder; beat white and sugar separate.

A Good Sponge Cake.
Mrs. Amelia Ohlwiler, Altoona.

4 eggs, 1 cup sugar, 1 cup flour, teaspoon Cleveland baking powder; beat the eggs very light, add sugar and beat more; flavor to taste.

Irish Rag Cake.

3 cups sugar, 1 cup butter, 5 eggs, 1 cup sweet milk, 3 cups flour, 3 teaspoons Cleveland baking powder.

Cocoanut Layer Cake.
Mrs. S. S. Herr, Pleasant Grove.

2 cups sugar, ½ cup butter, 3 eggs, 1 cup milk, 3 cups flour, 2 teaspoonfuls Cleveland baking powder.

Banana Cake.
Mrs. S. S. Herr, Pleasant Grove.

3 cups sugar, 3 cups flour, 1 cup sweet milk, 3 eggs, ½ cup butter, 3 teaspoons Cleveland baking powder. Slice the bananas and put on top of cake, it will melt the frosting if you put it between the layers.

Jelly Roll.
Mrs. John B. Fisher, Lancaster.

2 cups of sugar, 5 eggs, ½ cup of water, 2 cups of flour, 2 teaspoons of Cleveland baking powder.

Jelly.—1 lemon (grated), ½ cup of sugar, butter, size of a walnut; 1 egg; mix thoroughly and boil 3 minutes.

Cottolene requires only 2-3 the quantity of lard. Use it.

CAKES.

Sponge Cake.
Mrs. E. U. Sowers.

5 eggs, 1 pint of sugar, 1 pint of flour, and 5 tablespoons of water.

Sponge Cake.
Mrs. Ella D. Moore.

3 eggs, 2 cups sugar, 2 cups flour, ½ cup water, 2 teaspoonfuls of Cleveland baking powder.

Water Sponge Cake.
Mrs. Kohr.

2 cups sugar, 2 cups flour, 3 eggs, ½ cup warm water, 2 teaspoonfuls Cleveland baking powder.

Cocoanut Cake.
Mrs. Ella D. Moore.

¼ pound butter, 1 cocoanut, 1 pound sugar, 3 eggs, ½ pound flour.

Tip-top Cake.

1 pound of sugar, 1 cup of butter, 4 eggs, beaten separately; 1 cup of milk, 1 pound of chopped raisins, ½ pound of figs, chopped fine; ½ of a grated nutmeg, 2 teaspoons Cleveland baking powder, 1 pound of flour.

White Mountain Cake.
Laura Knipe.

3 cups of sugar, ¾ cups of butter, ½ cup of milk, 5 cups of flour, 5 eggs, 4 teaspoonfuls Cleveland baking powder; leave out 2 of the whites for icing.

Ice Cream Cake.
Mrs. Ella D. Moore.

¼ pound butter, 2 cups sugar, 2½ cups flour, 1 cup water, whites of 6 eggs, 3 teaspoons Cleveland baking powder.

Lemon Sponge Cake.
Mrs. M.

4 eggs, 2 cups granulated sugar, 2 cups sifted flour, 1 teaspoon Cleveland baking powder, 1 cup boiling milk, rind and juice of ½ lemon grated in batter—the other ½ for icing; beat eggs and sugar, then add flour and baking powder, and last, milk.

Cottolene requires only 2-3 the quantity of lard. Use it.

Tip-top Cake.

3 cups of flour, 2 cups of sugar, 1 cup sweet milk, large spoonful of butter, 2 teaspoonfuls of Cleveland baking powder and flavor to taste.

Plain Cake.
Mrs. S. P. Newhard, Philadelphia.

2 cups sugar, 2 eggs, 5 tablespoons butter, 2 cups sweet milk, 4 cups flour, 5 heaped teaspoons Cleveland baking powder, flavor with almond, vanilla or lemon

Cake That Never Fails.

2 cups sugar, ½ cup butter, 1 cup sweet milk, 3 cups flour, into which stir 2 teaspoons Cleveland baking powder, whites of 5 eggs, beaten to a froth. Beat butter and sugar to a cream, add milk and flour; stir eggs last. Flavor to taste.

Shoo-fly Cake.

½ cup sugar, ½ cup New Orleans molasses, 2 cups of flour, ½ teaspoon soda, ½ cup boiling water, lard enough to make flour and lard into rivels.

Goose Necks.
Mrs. J. Dewald.

1 cup sour cream, 1 cup butter, 2 cups sugar, 3 eggs, 1 teaspoonful baking soda, flour enough to roll out; sprinkle with sugar.

Cornucopia Cake.
Mrs. David Harpel.

2 cups sugar, ½ cup sweet milk, ½ cup butter, 2 cups flour, 4 eggs, 2 teaspoon Cleveland baking powder.

Delicious Cake.
Mrs. A. Hoover, West Fairview.

2 cups sugar, 2 cups flour, 6 eggs, 1 teaspoon Cleveland baking powder; beat the eggs and sugar very light, stir in flour and baking powder, sifted twice; bake in 3 deep tins.

Boiled frosting for cake.—Whites of 2 eggs, beaten to a stiff froth; 2 cups granulated sugar, ½ cup water; boil until thick as honey; pour the boiling syrup upon the beaten egg, with left hand beating hard, with right hand, add 1 tablespoon vanilla.

Cottolene requires only 2-3 the quantity of lard. Use it.

Picnic Cake.

3 eggs, 1 cup of butter, 2 cups of sugar, 1 cup of sweet milk, 3 cups of flour, 1 teaspoonful of soda, 2 teaspoonfuls of cream of tartar.

Graham Cake.
Mrs. John T. Atkins.

2 cups of sugar, ½ cup of butter, 3 cups of flour, 1 cup of sweet milk, 3 eggs, 3 teaspoons Cleveland baking powder.

Plain Cake.
Mrs. Clark.

3 cups sugar, 1 cup sweet milk, ½ cup butter, 4 cups of flour, 4 eggs, 3 teaspoon Cleveland baking powder.

Dutch Cake.
Mrs. Lape.

3 cups of sugar, ¾ of a cup of butter, 6 eggs, 2 cups of sweet milk, 5 cups of flour, 5 teaspoonful Cleveland baking powder.

Lemon Jelly Cake.

½ cup sugar, 2 cups flour, ½ cup thick milk, ½ cup butter, 3 eggs, a little soda. To make the jelly, 1 cup sugar, 1 egg, small piece butter, the rind and juice of 1 lemon.

Cake of '76.
Mrs. John T. Atkins.

3 cups of sugar, 1 cup of butter, 1 cup of sour milk, 3 cups of flour, 6 eggs, 1 tablespoon cream of tartar, 1 teaspoon soda.

Imperial Cake.
Mrs. Ira Rutter.

1 pound butter, 1 pound sugar, 1 pound flour, 9 eggs, 1 lemon, grated rind and juice; 1¼ pounds almonds, before broken; ½ pound citron, ½ pound seedless raisins. Cream butter and sugar, then add yolks of eggs beaten light, then the whites, beaten; lastly the flour, reserving part for the fruit and nuts, which must be blanched and cut fine; 1½ teaspoons powder with flour.

Feather Cake.
Mrs. John H. Diehl.

2 cups sugar, ½ cup butter, 2-3 cup milk, 3 cups flour, 5 eggs, flavor with lemon or vanilla.

Cottolene requires only 2-3 the quantity of lard. Use it.

Currant Cake.
Mrs. Brunner.

1 pound of currants, 1 pound of raisins, 1 cup of butter, 1 cup of sugar, 1 cup of molasses, 4 cups of flour, 3 eggs, 2 tablespoons Cleveland baking powder.

Molasses Cake.
Mrs. Clark.

2 cups molasses, 1 cup sour milk, $\frac{1}{2}$ cup shortening; flour to thicken.

Rochester Cake.
Mrs. M. H. Parker.

2 cups sugar, 3 cups flour, 1 cup sweet milk, $\frac{3}{4}$ cup butter, 3 eggs, beaten separately; 3 teaspoonfuls Cleveland baking powder, 1 cup raisins, 1 nutmeg, 1 tablespoonful of cinnamon. Bake either in layers or loaf.

Duchess Cake.

$1\frac{1}{2}$ cups butter, 1 cup sugar, 6 eggs, 1 teaspoonful of Cleveland baking powder; mix with 1 pint flour, 1 teaspoonful of cinnamon. Rub butter and sugar to light cream, add eggs, 2 at a time, beating well between each; mix into a medium thick batter. Bake 30 minutes; take from the oven and ice.

Washington Cake.
Mrs. John H. Diehl.

$1\frac{1}{2}$ pounds sugar, $1\frac{3}{4}$ pounds flour, $\frac{3}{4}$ pound butter, 1 pint milk, 10 eggs, 1 nutmeg, 1 teaspoon cloves, 1 pound currants, 1 pound raisins, 1 teaspoon soda, dissolved in boiling water.

White Cake.
Mrs. H. T. Atkins.

Whites of 8 eggs, 2 cups of sugar, not quite a cup of butter, not quite a cup of cornstarch, scant quart of flour, 2 teaspoons Cleveland baking powder, 1 cup sweet milk. Flavor with almond.

French Cake.
Mrs. S. S. Boltz.

2 cups sugar, 2 cups flour, 1 cup sweet milk, $\frac{1}{2}$ cup butter, 4 eggs, 3 teaspoons Cleveland baking powder.

Cottolene requires only 2-3 the quantity of lard. Use it.

CAKES. 147

White Loaf.

Whites of 8 eggs, 2 cups of powdered sugar, ½ cup butter, ¾ cup sweet milk, 3 cups of flour, 2 teaspoons Cleveland baking powder. Cream butter and sugar, then add milk, the whites of eggs, beaten very stiff, and the flour; stir very hard. Flavor this if you like.

Centennial Cake.
Mrs. J. H. Roberts.

White part.—1 cup sweet milk, 3 eggs, 2 cups white sugar, ½ cup butter, 1 teaspoon cream of tartar, 1 teaspoon soda, 2 teaspoons flour; flavor with nutmeg or lemon.

Dark part.—1 cup brown sugar, ½ cup butter, ½ cup molasses, ¼ cup strong coffee, 2½ cups flour, 2 eggs,.1 cup raisins. Spice to suit the taste. Take the white of 1 egg and beat it with sugar and spread them as you lay them together; put the yellow in the dark.

Fairy Queen Cake.
Vivian Hummel.

The whites of 4 eggs, 1 cup of milk, ½ cup of shortening, 1 cup of sugar, 2½ cups of flour, 2 teaspoonfuls Cleveland baking powder. Cream the shortening and sugar, add milk, and sift in the flour and baking powder; beat the whites of the eggs and add them the last; flavor to taste with a teaspoonful or lemon or vanilla.

Crust Cake
Mrs. I. M. Hean.

2 cups sugar, 2½ cups flour, 2 teaspoonfuls Cleveland baking powder, 2 eggs, 1 cup milk, butter, size of an egg; add a little vanilla and bake on crust; sprinkle well with pulverized sugar before baking.

Jam Cake.
Mrs. Regan, Elmwood, Ill.

1 cup of jam, ½ cup of butter, 1 cup sugar, 3 eggs, 1 teaspoonful cinnamon, 1 teaspoonful allspice, ½ teaspoonful cloves, ½ teaspoonful grated nutmeg, 1 teaspoonful of soda, 4 tablespoonfuls of sour milk, 1¾ cups of flour. Bake in 2 layers; finish with icing.

Cottolene requires only 2-3 the quantity of lard. Use it.

Lemon Cake.
Mrs. Jacob Karch.

1 pound sugar, 1 pound flour, 6 ounces of butter, 1 tumbler of sweet milk, 5 eggs, beat separately; 1 teaspoon of soda, 1 teaspoon of cream of tartar; flavor with lemon; bake in pound cake dish.

French Cake.
Mrs. W. Klopp.

3 cups of sugar, 4 eggs, 1 scant cup of butter, 1 cup of sweet milk, 3 heaped cups flour, 2 teaspoonfuls Cleveland baking powder, 2 teaspoonfuls vanilla. Beat sugar, eggs and butter to a cream, then add milk; stir lightly after flour and powder are added.

French Cake.
Mrs. J. H. Roberts.

1 cup of butter, 2 cups of sugar, 3 cups of flour, 1 cup of milk, 1 teaspoonful of Cleveland baking powder, flavor to taste, whites of 4 eggs. Cream the butter, add sugar, then the milk, then flour, then eggs.

Velvet Cake.
Esther E. Grow, Phoenixville.

4 eggs, 1 pound pulverized sugar, 1 pound flour, 1 teaspoonful Cleveland baking powder, sifted with flour; $\frac{1}{2}$ pound butter, 1 cup of cold water; beat butter and sugar to a cream, add the cold water, beat the eggs separately, then together 1 minute, then add eggs and flour alternately.

Vanity Cake.
Olivia S. Hinman, Battle Creek, Mich.

$1\frac{1}{2}$ cups sugar, $\frac{1}{2}$ cup butter, $\frac{1}{2}$ cup sweet milk, $1\frac{1}{2}$ cups flour, 2 cups corn starch, teaspoon Cleveland baking powder, whites of 6 eggs; bake in 2 layers, putting frosting between and on top.

Silver Cake.
Mrs. David Harpel.

$\frac{1}{2}$ cup of butter, 2 cups sugar, whites of 8 eggs, $\frac{3}{4}$ cup milk, $2\frac{1}{2}$ cups sifted flour, $\frac{1}{2}$ teaspoon soda, 1 teaspoon cream of tartar, 1 tablespoon extract of almond.

Cottolene requires only 2-3 the quantity of lard. Use it.

Walnut Cake.
Mrs. W. D. Zehnder.

1 coffee cupful of sugar, 2 of raisins (stoned and chopped), 1½ cupfuls of flour, ½ cupful of butter, ½ cupful of sweet milk, 3 eggs, 2 teaspoonfuls of Cleveland baking powder, ½ nutmeg, grated; 1 teaspoonful of lemon or vanilla, 1 cup heaping full of nuts, which must be cracked and picked, before anything else is done to the cake. Bake slowly, with a buttered paper in the bottom of tin.

Minnehaha Cake.
Mrs. S. B. Cox.

2 cupfuls of sugar, ½ a cupful of butter, 1 cupful of milk, the whites of 6 eggs, 3 cupfuls of flour, 3 teaspoonfuls of Cleveland baking powder; bake in layers. Make the frosting as follows: 2 cupfuls of granulated sugar, and whites of 2 eggs; pour 5 or 6 teaspoonfuls of boiling water over sugar and let it boil 3 or 4 minutes until it stands when poured from a spoon. Pour over the whites, which have been beaten to a stiff froth; pour the sugar on slowly, beating until cool; mix with this 1 cupful small raisins, 1 cupful English walnuts; spread between the layers and on top.

Railroad Cake.
Mrs. John Killian.

1 cup of sugar, 1 cup of flour, 3 eggs, a pinch of soda, mixed with the flour. Beat the sugar and eggs 15 minutes. Bake in a quick oven.

Railroad Cake.
Mrs. S. S. Boltz.

2 cups sugar, ½ cup butter, 1 cup sweet milk, 3 eggs, 3 cups flour, 3 teaspoonfuls Cleveland baking powder; sieve baking powder and flour 4 times.

Rochester Cake.
Mrs. I. M. Hean.

3 eggs, ½ cup butter, 1 cup milk, 2 cups of sugar, 3 cups of flour, 1 cup raisins, chopped fine; 2 teaspoonfuls of cinnamon, 1 teaspoonful of cloves, 1 nutmeg, 2 teaspoonfuls Cleveland baking powder. Bake in layers and ice.

Cottolene requires only 2-3 the quantity of lard. Use it.

Silver Cake.
Mrs. Amanda Fry, Pleasant Grove.

1½ cups of sugar, ½ cup of butter, ¾ of a cup of sweet milk, whites of 4 eggs, 2½ cups of flour, 2 teaspoons of Cleveland baking powder.

Thumb Cake.
Mrs. John H. Diehl.

1 cup sugar, a piece of butter, the size of your thumb; beat sugar and butter to a cream, add 2 well beaten eggs, ½ cup milk, 1½ cups flour, 2 teaspoons cream of tartar, 1 teaspoon soda; bake in 2 layers.

Mrs. Sherman's Cake.
Mrs. J. Dewald.

2 cups sugar, 1 cup sweet milk, 1 cup butter, ½ cup corn starch in the milk, 2½ cups flour, 4 eggs, 2 teaspoons of Cleveland baking powder.

Jenny Lind Cake.
Mrs. Chas. H. Rockel, Allentown.

1 cup sugar, ½ cup butter, ½ cup milk, 1½ cups flour, 2 eggs, 2 teaspoons Cleveland baking powder.

Bride Cake.
H. M. M.

1½ cups pulverized sugar, ½ cup butter, 1 cup sweet milk, ¼ cup corn starch, 2 cups of flour, whites of 3 eggs, 2 teaspoons Cleveland baking powder.

Lincoln Cake.
Mrs. Robt. Hean.

2 cups sugar, 3 cups flour, ½ cup butter, 1 cup milk, 2 eggs, 2 teaspoonfuls Cleveland baking powder. Bake in layers.

Pearl Cake.
Mrs. John T. Atkins.

2 cups of sugar, ½ cup of corn starch, 2½ cups of flour, ¾ cup of butter, 1 cup of sweet milk, 2 teaspoons of Cleveland baking powder, whites of 5 eggs.

Orange Cake.
Mrs. S. S. Boltz.

2 cups sugar, 2 cups flour, ½ cup water, 5 eggs, 2 teaspoons Cleveland baking powder, 1 orange.

Cottolene requires only 2-3 the quantity of lard. Use it.

CAKES.

Cream Cake.

1 teaspoonful of soda and 1 teaspoon of cream of tartar, dissolved in 1 cup of sour cream; add 1 cup of sugar and enough flour to make a very stiff batter. Put in pie pans and before baking take butter, size of a walnut; 2 tablespoons of sugar, and a little cinnamon; mix and spread on top.

Fig Cake.
Mrs. Walter Randall, Tamaqua.

1½ cups of sugar, ¾ cup of butter (scant measure), whites of 5 eggs, ½ cup of milk, 2 teaspoonfuls of Cleveland baking powder, 2 cups of flour; bake in layers. Make boiled icing and put in 1 cup of finely chopped figs.

Cheap Cream Cake.
Mrs. Chance.

1 cup of sugar, 1 egg, 1 cup of sweet milk, 2 cups of flour, 1 tablespoonful of butter; cream sugar and butter, add egg and beat light, add milk and flour and 2 teaspoonfuls Cleveland baking powder; flavor with vanilla; bake in layers.

Cream for filling.—Beat 1 egg, ½ cup of sugar together, then add ¼ cup of flour, wet with very little milk, stir into ½ pint boiling milk; cook until thick; flavor with vanilla; spread the cream when cool between the cakes.

Lady Cake.
Miss Hattie Bickel.

2 cups of sugar, 1 cup of butter, 1 cup of sweet milk, 3 cups of flour, 3 cups of Cleveland baking powder, whites of 8 eggs; flavor with bitter almonds.

Orange Cake.
Mrs. Chance.

2 cups of sugar, ½ cup of butter, stirred to a cream; 1 cup of sweet milk, 3 eggs, well beaten; 3 cups of sifted flour, 2 teaspoonfuls of Cleveland baking powder. Bake in sheets or layers.

Icing.—Take ½ pound of pulverized sugar, put in a bowl and grate the yellow of 1 orange and add 1 large tablespoonful of boiling water and stir together, then add enough juice so it will spread nicely.

Cottolene requires only 2-3 the quantity of lard. Use it.

Pearl Cake.
Mrs. A. M. Thomas.

Whites of 5 eggs, 2 cups pulverized sugar, 1 cup butter; work to cream; 1 cup sweet milk, 2 cups flour, 1 cup corn starch, 2 teaspoons Cleveland baking powder; flavor with vanilla.

Orange Cake.
Mrs. Light.

4 cups sugar, 8 eggs; beat yolks and sugar very light, then add the whites of 6, and 4 cups of flour, 3 teaspoons Cleveland baking powder, 2 oranges, grated; last, 1 cup of boiling water.

Lady Cake.
Mrs. S. G. Valentine.

Mix 2 cups sugar and 1 cup butter until very light, add gradually 1 cup sweet milk, 4 cups of flour, 2 large teaspoons Cleveland baking powder, 3 teaspoons bitter almond; add last, beaten whites of 10 eggs. Makes 1 large or 2 small cakes.

Black Cake.
Jennie McLain.

2 cups brown sugar, 1 cup butter, 1 cup sour milk, 1 cup of raisins, 1 cup currants, 2 eggs, 3 cups flour, a small tablespoon soda, dissolved in hot water; 1 tablespoon cinnamon, 1 teaspoon cloves, 1 teaspoon allspice, ½ nutmeg. You can vary the spices to suit taste; citron improves it.

Black Cake.
Mrs. W. H. Newhard, Allentown.

½ cup butter, 1 cup sour milk, 2 cups brown sugar, 2 eggs, 3 cups flour, 1 cup raisins (seeded), ½ teaspoonful nutmeg, ½ teaspoonful cinnamon, ¼ teaspoonful cloves, a small teaspoonful soda and cream of tartar.

Mock Lady Cake.

Whites of 6 eggs, 2 cups of sugar, ¾ cup of butter; beat sugar and butter to a cream; 1 cup of sweet milk, 3 teaspoonfuls Cleveland baking powder; beat the whites of the eggs in last. Flavor to your own taste.

Cottolene requires only 2-3 the quantity of lard. Use it.

CAKES.

Jelly Cake.
Mrs. A. M. Ayers.

2 cups soft white sugar, 3 cups flour, 1 cup butter, 1 cup thick milk, 5 eggs, 1 teaspoonful of baking soda; bake in layers and spread with jelly.

Hildebrand Cake.
Mrs. Robt. Hean.

2 cups sugar, ¾ cup butter and lard mixed, 3½ cups of flour, 3 eggs, 2 teaspoonfuls baking soda, 1 cup sweet milk.

Queen of Beauty Cake.
Mrs. R. S. Spotten.

1 pound of A sugar, 1 cup of butter, 1 cup of milk, 3½ cups of flour, well sifted; the whites of 5 eggs, 3 teaspoons of Cleveland baking powder, 1 teaspoon of almond extract; mix butter and sugar to a cream, then add the milk and flour with the baking powder, then add the whites of eggs, well beaten; divide the batter into 2 parts; to the one half add a ½ teaspoon of raspberry coloring. This fills 4 jelly tins.

For the Icing.—The whites of 2 eggs, beaten to a stiff froth; boil 1 pound of A sugar and a ½ cup of water until it pulls, then pour over the whites of the eggs and stir until cool; spread on cakes, putting together, first white, then pink; add a ½ teaspoon of the coloring to the icing.

Orange Cake.
Mrs. R. S. Malsberger.

The grated rind and juice of 1 large orange, 5 eggs, 2 cups of pulverized sugar; beat the 3 together ½ hour, add ½ cup cold water, 2 teaspoons of Cleveland baking powder, and 2 cups of flour sifted together; bake as a layer cake; flavor the icing with orange.

Brown Coffee Cakes.
Mrs. John Urich.

1 cup of butter, 2 cups of brown sugar, 1 cup of dark molasses, 3 eggs, 1 cup of strong coffee, 5 cups of flour, 1 pound seeded raisins, ½ pound citron, orange and lemon peel mixed, ½ nutmeg, grated; ½ teaspoon of cinnamon, ¼ teaspoon of ground cloves, 1 heaping teaspoon soda.

Cottolene requires only 2-3 the quantity of lard. Use it.

Orange Cake.
Mrs. R. H. Graeff.

2 cups white sugar, yolks of 5 eggs, whites of 2 eggs, ½ cup water, 2 cups flour, 2 teaspoons Cleveland baking powder, the juice and grated rind of 1 orange, a pinch of salt. Bake in tins. (Batter between the cakes.)

Beat whites of 2 eggs to a stiff froth, 7 large tablespoons of powdered sugar, grated rind and juice of 1 orange.

Orange Cake.
Mrs. Foltz.

1 pound sugar, ½ pound of butter, 8 eggs, 1 pound of flour; bake in layers. Whites of 2 of the eggs and pulverized sugar make a stiff icing, and use the juice of orange and grated rind.

Buckeye Cake.

6 eggs, 1 pound of sugar, 1 cup of sweet milk, 1 cup of butter, 1 teaspoon of soda, 1 of cream of tartar, 4½ cups of flour.

Number Cake.

1 cup of butter, 1 cup of sour milk, 2 cups of sugar, 3 cups of flour, 5 eggs, 2 teaspoons of cream of tartar, 1 teaspoon of soda, 1 nutmeg.

Snowball Cake.

1½ cups of butter, 1 cup of loaf sugar, whites of 3 eggs, 1 teaspoon of soda. Bake in small cakes.

Minute Cake.

1 egg, 1 cup of sugar, ½ cup of butter, ¾ cup of milk, 1 teaspoonful of soda, 2½ cups of flour. Bake in long pan.

Puff Cakes.
Katherine Louser.

2½ cups sugar, ½ cup butter, 3 eggs, 3 cups flour, 1 cup milk, 1½ teaspoonfuls Cleveland baking powder; flavor to taste.

One-egg Cake.
Mrs. C. Shiner.

½ cup of butter, 1 cup of sugar, 1 well beaten egg, 1 scant cup of milk, 2 even cups of flour, 2 even teaspoons of Cleveland baking powder, 1 teaspoonful of lemon or vanilla. Bake in a shallow pan in a moderate oven ½ hour.

Cottolene requires only 2-3 the quantity of lard. Use it.

CAKES.

Poor Man's Cake.
Mrs. Henry Cole, Allentown.

1 cup sugar, 1 cup molasses, 1 cup butter and lard, 1 teaspoon soda, 4 cups flour, 1 cup water.

White Cake.

½ cup butter and 1 cup of sugar, stirred to a cream. Then stir into that ½ cup of milk and 1½ cupfuls flour, 2 teaspoonfuls of Cleveland baking powder having been stirred into it, lastly add the well beaten whites of 4 eggs. Can be baked in layers or solid.

Mixture for Filling.—Boil 1½ cupfuls sugar until it candies, then stir this into the well beaten whites of 2 eggs.

1, 2, 3, 4 Cake.

2 cups granulated sugar, 1 cup butter, 1 cup sweet milk, 4 cups flour, 4 eggs, 1 small teaspoon cream of tartar, 1 small teaspoon soda, 1½ cups of raisins, cut and flour before putting in cake; flavor with lemon or nutmeg; bake in 2 loaf pans.

Caramel Cake.
Mrs. Miles Ganoe.

1 cup of butter, 2 cup of sugar, 1 scant cup of milk, 1½ cups of flour, 1 cup corn starch, whites of 4 eggs, 3 teaspoonfuls of Cleveland baking powder in the flour. Bake in a long pan.

Dover Cake.

1 pound of granulated sugar, ½ pound of butter, 6 eggs, 1 cup of thick milk, 1 pound of flour, sifted; 1 teaspoon of soda, 2 teaspoons of Cream of tartar, flavor to taste. Work sugar and butter together to a cream; beat whites of eggs and also yolks separately very light; dissolve soda in the thick milk, put the cream of tartar in the flour.

Spice Cake.
Mrs. Rev. I. C. Fisher.

2 cups of brown sugar, ½ cup melted butter, 4 eggs, take the whites of 2 of them for icing; 3 cups of flour, 1 cup of sour milk, 1 nutmeg, 2 teaspoons cinnamon, 1½ teaspoons cloves, 1 teaspoon soda. Bake in 4 layers.

Cottolene requires only 2-3 the quantity of lard. Use it.

Dover Cake.
Mrs. C. Shiner.

2½ cups sugar, 1 cup butter, 1 cup sweet milk, 1 cup corn starch, 2½ cups flour, 3½ spoons Cleveland baking powder, the whites of 5 eggs, flavor with lemon or vanilla.

Snowflake Cake.

2 cups sugar, 1 cup of butter, 1 cup sweet milk, 1 cup corn starch, 2 cups flour, 2 teaspoons Cleveland baking powder; add lastly the whites of 6 eggs, beaten stiff.

Orange Cake.
Mrs. J. D. Keefer, Columbia.

2½ cups of sugar, 1 cup of butter, 1 cup of sweet milk, 1½ teaspoonfuls of Cleveland baking powder, 4 cups of flour, 4 eggs. Bake in layers.

Icing for above.—2 cups of sugar, 1 cup of water; add together and boil until it makes a stiff syrup; whites of 2 eggs; beat stiff, then add the syrup to eggs; pour syrup slow, the thickness of a straw, and beat well while pouring; flavor with outside of an orange (grated).

Orange Cake.
Elma A. Fry, Pleasant Grove.

1½ cups sugar, 2-3 cup butter, 2½ cups flour, 2 teaspoons cream of tartar, 1 teaspoon soda, 1 cup of milk, whites of 5 eggs; bake in 4 tins.

(Custard for same.)

1 orange, juice, rind and pulp; ½ juice of a lemon, 1 cup of pulverized sugar, yolks of 5 eggs; boil slowly until it will thicken; when cold spread between layers.

Spice Cake.

2 pounds brown sugar, 1 cup butter, 1 cup sour cream, 3 cups flour, 2 eggs, 1 teaspoon soda, 1 teaspoon each of cloves, cinnamon, allspice, nutmeg, ginger. Bake in layers.

Corn Starch Cake.
Mrs. John J. Bowman.

3 cups sugar, 1 of butter, 4 eggs, 1 cup corn starch, 1 cup milk, 3 cups flour, 1 teaspoon Cleveland baking powder.

Cottolene requires only 2-3 the quantity of lard. Use it.

CAKES.

Corn Starch Cake.
Mrs. David Harpel.

Whites of 3 eggs, 1 cup white sugar, 1-3 cup butter, ½ cup milk, 1 cup flour, 1 cup corn starch, 1 teaspoon soda, 2 teaspoons cream of tartar; flavor with lemon or vanilla.

Guess Cake.
Mrs. R. G. Stanley.

2 cups of white sugar, ½ cup of butter, 3 eggs, 1 cup of sweet milk, 2½ cups of flour, 1 teaspoon of soda, 2 teaspoons of cream of tartar.

Love Cake.

1½ cups sugar, ¾ cup butter, 3 eggs, ½ cup sweet milk, 2½ cups flour, 1½ Cleveland baking powder, 1½ soda, ½ cocoanut, sugar, butter, yellow of eggs.

Vanilla Cake.
Mrs. S. P. Newhard, Philadelphia.

1½ cups sugar, 1-3 cup butter, 3 eggs, ½ cup milk, 2 cups of flour, 2 teaspoons Cleveland baking powder. Bake in layers.

Filling for same.—½ cup flour, 1 cup sugar, 2 eggs, well beaten; stir into a pint of milk while boiling; flavor with vanilla.

Crumb Cake.
Mrs. Kohr.

6 cups of flour, 3 cups of sugar, 1 cup of butter, 2 eggs, 1 teaspoon soda, 1 teaspoon cream of tartar.

Moss Cake.
Katie Kaufman.

2 cups of sugar, ½ cup of butter, 1 cup of sweet milk, 2½ cups of flour; beat 2 eggs, 2 teaspoons of Cleveland baking powder; flavor with vanilla. Split cake on layers and fill with sauce.

Sauce for cake.—1 pint of sweet milk, boil and boil, add 1 tablespoon of corn starch, 2 tablespoons of sugar, 1 egg; let all come to a boil, and flavor with vanilla.

Moss Cake.
Mrs. S. Reinoehl.

2½ cups sugar, 1 cup sweet milk, ¾ cup butter, 2½ cups flour, 3 eggs, 3 tablespoonfuls Cleveland baking powder.

Cottolene requires only 2-3 the quantity of lard. Use it.

Fruit Cake.
Mrs. A. Gates.

2 scant teacupfuls of butter, 3 cupfuls of dark brown sugar, 6 eggs, whites and yolks beaten separately; 1 pound of raisins, seeded; 1 of currants, washed and dried; ½ a pound of citron, cut in thin strips; also ½ a cupful of cooking molasses, ½ a cupful of sour milk. Stir the butter and sugar to a cream, add to that ½ a grated nutmeg, 1 tablespoonful of ground cinnamon, 1 teaspoonful of cloves, 1 teaspoonful of mace; add the molasses and sour milk. Stir all well; then put in the beaten yolks of eggs; stir again all thoroughly, and then add 4 cupfuls of sifted flour, alternately with the beaten whites of eggs. Now dissolve a level teaspoonful of soda, and stir in thoroughly. Mix the fruit together, and stir into it 2 heaping tablespoonfuls flour; then stir it in the cake. Butter baking tins carefully, line them with letter paper well buttered, and bake in a moderate oven; if in 1 large pan, bake 3 hours; if in 2 common-sized pans, 2 hours.

Fruit Cake.
Mrs. Edgar Lamoreaux.

4 cups brown sugar, 1 cup molasses, 2 cups butter, 1 cup sour milk, 1 pound currants, 1 pound raisins, ½ pound citron, 6 eggs, beaten; 1 tablespoonful cinnamon, 1 tablespoonful cloves, 1 tablespoonful allspice, 2 teaspoonfuls salaratus, and then the flour.

Fruit Cake.
Mrs. John H. Diehl.

3 pounds sugar, 3 pounds butter, 3 pounds flour, 30 eggs, 6 pounds currants, 6 pounds raisins, 1 pound citron, 1 ounce mace, 1 ounce nutmeg.

Fruit Cake.
H. M. M.

4 cups of brown sugar, 1 cup of dark molasses, 2 cups of butter, 10 cups of flour, 8 eggs, 1 cup cherry preserves, 1 pound of almonds, 2 lemons, grated; 2 nutmegs, 2 tablespoons of soda, 1 tablespoon of cloves, 1 tablespoon of ginger, ½ pint of sour cream, 4 pounds of raisins, 4 pounds of currants, 1 pound of citron, 1 pound of figs.

Cottolene requires only 2-3 the quantity of lard. Use it.

Tea Cake.

2½ cups sugar, 2½ cups flour, 2½ spoons Cleveland baking powder, 1 cup sweet milk, ½ cup butter, 3 eggs, beaten light and separately.

Scotch Cake.
Mrs. Dr. Dechart.

1 pound sugar, ¼ cup cold water, ½ cup shortening, 2 eggs, 1 teaspoon cinnamon, 1 teaspoon allspice, 1 teaspoon cloves, 1 teaspoon soda.

Cream Cake.
Mrs. S. Dewald.

1 cup of butter, 2 cups of sugar, 1 cup of sweet milk, 1 tablespoon soda, 1 tablespoon cream of tartar, 3½ cups of flour, 4 eggs, the whites beaten separately; flavor to taste and put the cream between the layers when cold.

Cream.—2-3 cup of sugar, 1½ cups of sweet milk, 1½ tablespoons of corn starch, 2 eggs, reserving the whites for icing.

Fruit Cake.
Mrs. Ira Rutter.

3 cups sugar, 1 cup butter, 5 cups flour, 1 cup cream or milk, 1 nutmeg, 1 lemon and 1 orange, 1 teaspoon soda, 1 cup cold coffee, 1 cup N. O. molasses, 1 pound dates, ½ pound figs, 1 pound raisins, 1 pound currants, ½ pound citron. Bake 3 hours.

White Fruit Cake.
Mrs. J. J. Newhard.

¾ pound citron, 1 pound shellbark kernels, ½ pound white sugar, 1 pound butter, 1 pound flour, 1 pound seedless raisins, 6 eggs, 1 cup sweet milk, 1½ teaspoons vanilla, 2½ teaspoons Cleveland baking powder, 1 cocoanut. The fruit must all be chopped fine and dusted with flour and added last; scald the almonds to remove the skins; ¾ pound chopped almonds required.

Tea Cake.

1 cup of sugar, 1 egg, ¼ cup of butter, 1-3 cup of sweet milk, 1 coffee cup of flour, 1½ teaspoonfuls of Cleveland baking powder; flavor to suit taste.

Cottolene requires only 2-3 the quantity of lard. Use it.

Fruit Cake by Measure.
Mary A. Railton.

2 scant teacupfuls of butter, 3 cupfuls of dark brown sugar, 6 eggs, whites and yolks beaten separately; 1 pound of raisins (seeded), 1 of currants, washed and dried; ½ a pound of citron, cut in thin strips; also ¼ a cupful of cooking molasses, ½ a cupful of sour milk. Stir the butter and sugar to a cream, add to that ½ a grated nutmeg, 1 tablespoonful of ground cinnamon, 1 teaspoonful of cloves, 1 teaspoonful of mace; add the molasses and sour milk. Stir all well; then put in the beaten yolks of eggs; stir all thoroughly; then add 4 cupfuls of sifted flour, alternately with the beaten whites of egg. Now dissolve a level teaspoonful of soda and stir in thoroughly; mix the fruit together and stir into it 2 heaping tablespoonfuls of flour; then stir it in the cake. Butter 2 common-sized baking tins carefully, line them with letter paper, well buttered, and bake in a moderate oven 2 hours. After it is baked let it cool in the pan; after that put into a tight can.

Fruit Cake.
Mrs. L.

2 cups pulverized sugar, 2 cups butter, 8 eggs, 1½ pints flour, 3 cups currants, 1½ raisins, 1½ citron, 1 cup candied lemon and orange peel, 1 cup blanched almonds, ½ ounce nutmeg, mace, and cinnamon, ½ tablespoon allspice and cloves. Rub butter and sugar together, then eggs, beaten separately; then fruit in flour; use 4 quart pan.

Gold Cake.
Mrs. Kohr.

2 cups sugar, 1 cup butter, 1 cup sweet milk, 4 cups flour, yolks of 8 eggs, 2 teaspoons Cleveland baking powder.

Gold Loaf Cake.
Mrs. John H. Diehl.

Yolks of 8 eggs, 1 cup granulated sugar, ½ cup butter, ½ cup sweet milk, 1½ cups flour, 2 teaspoons Cleveland baking powder; cream butter and sugar thoroughly, beat yolks to a stiff froth, put in milk, then flour and beat hard; bake in a tube pan in a moderate oven.

Cottolene requires only 2-3 the quantity of lard. Use it.

Cheap Fruit Cake.
Mrs. Chas. H. Rockel, Allentown.

1 cup butter, ¾ pound sugar, 1 cup milk, 4 eggs, 4 cups flour, 1 pound currants, 1 pound raisins, ½ pound citron, 1 teapoon nutmeg, 1 teaspoon cloves, 1 teaspoon cinnamon, 1 teaspoon ginger, 1 teaspoon allspice, 1 teaspoon soda or 2 heaping teaspoons Cleveland baking powder; dredge your fruit with flour, and add just before baking.

Hickorynut Cake.
Mrs. S. S. Herr, Pleasant Grove.

½ cup butter, 2 cups sugar, 4 eggs, beaten separately; 3 cups flour, ½ cup sweet milk, 2 teaspoonfuls Cleveland baking powder, 2 teaspoonfuls vanilla, 2 cups hickory nuts. Mix baking powder with flour, put 1 cup of chopped nuts in the cake, the other cupful leave in halves and stick on top of the frosting.

Fruit Cake.
Sallie Southan.

½ pound brown sugar, ½ pound butter, ¼ pound citron, 4 eggs, ½ nutmeg, 1 pound currants, 1 pound raisins, 1 tablespoon cinnamon, 1 heaping tablespoon cloves, 1 teaspoon baking soda, 1 teaspoon cream of tartar, a little salt, 1 gill milk, flour enough.

Old Black Joe Cake.
Mrs. J. Dewald.

1 cup of sugar, ½ cup of butter, ½ cup of milk, 2 cups flour, 2 eggs, 2 teaspoonfuls of Cleveland baking powder, ½ cake of chocolate, ½ cup of milk, yolk of 1 egg, 1 cupful of sugar, 1 Boil the last 5 things together and then mix with the rest; boil just until it gets a little bit thick. Ice it just as you would any other cake. We generally use the boiled icing.

Hickorynut Cake.
Mrs. Billingham.

1 cup butter, 2 cups of sugar, 1 cup of sweet milk, 3 eggs, whites and yolks beaten separately; 1 pint of hickorynut kernels, chopped fine; 1 pint of currants and 1 pint of raisins; mix and add 5 cups of flour, having in it 3 teaspoonfuls of Cleveland baking powder.

Cottolene requires only 2-3 the quantity of lard. Use it.

Gold Cake.
Mrs. M. B. Smith.

Yolks of 10 eggs, 2 cups sugar, ½ cup butter, 1 teaspoon soda, 2 teaspoons cream of tartar, 1 cup sweet milk, 3½ cups flour.

Gold Cake.
Mrs. David Harpel.

1 cup sugar, ½ cup butter, 1-3 teaspoon soda in ½ teacup of sweet milk, yolks of 5 eggs, 2 cups flour, 1-3 teaspoon cream of tartar, mixed in flour with vanilla.

Gold Cake.
Mrs. Ella D. Moore.

2 cups sugar, 1 cup milk, 1 cup butter, 4 cups flour, yolks of 4 eggs, 1 teaspoonful soda, 2 teaspoonfuls cream of tartar.

Delicious Cake.
Mrs. Chance.

1 cup of sugar, ½ cup of butter, 2 eggs, the yolks and whites separately beaten; ½ cup of milk, 1½ cups of flour and ½ teaspoonful of Cleveland baking powder; cream sugar and butter, add the yolks and milk; sift flour and baking powder, and stir all together; then add the whites of eggs last and bake.

Delicious Cake.
Laura Knipe.

2 cups of sugar, 1 cup of lard, mixed to a cream; 3 cups of flour, 1 cup of milk, 4 eggs, beat each part separately; 3 teaspoonfuls of Cleveland baking powder, and flavoring if desired.

Delicious Cake.

2 cups sugar, ½ cup butter, ¾ cup sweet milk, 2½ cups sifted flour, whites of 8 eggs, beaten stiff; cream the butter and sugar, then add the milk and flour, in which 2 teaspoons Cleveland baking powder have been mixed; whites of eggs last; use pulverized sugar.

Nut Cake.
Mrs. Chas. H. Rockel, Allentown.

1½ cups sugar, ½ cup butter, ¾ cup sweet milk, ¾ cup nuts, whites of 4 eggs, 2 teaspoons Cleveland baking powder, 2 cups flour.

Cottolene requires only 2-3 the quantity of lard. Use it.

CAKES.

Gold and Silver Cake.
Mrs. Chas. H. Rockel, Allentown.

Beat 1 cup butter and 2 cups sugar together; add 1 cup milk, 4 cups flour, 4 teaspoons Cleveland baking powder; mix all together, then separate and add beaten whites of 5 eggs to $\frac{1}{2}$, and yolks to the remainder.

Fruit Cake.
Mrs. K. H. Mish.

3 cups sugar, 1 cup butter, 1 cup sour cream or thick milk. 6 eggs, 4 cups flour, 1 teaspoonful soda, 1 nutmeg, 2 pounds raisins, 2 pounds currants, $\frac{1}{2}$ pound citron, the rind and juice of 1 lemon. Bake 2 hours.

Nut Cake.
Mrs. John H. Diehl.

2 cups sugar, 1 cup butter, 3 cups flour, 1 cup milk, 3 eggs, beaten lightly, 2 teaspoons Cleveland baking powder, 1 cup currants; bake in jelly cake pans; put nut kernels in icing.

Nut Cake.
Mrs. J. Dewald.

1 cup of butter, 6 eggs, 1 pound of sugar; work this to a cream; 1 cup sweet milk, 1 teaspoon cream of tartar, 1 teaspoon soda, 4 cups of flour, 1 pint of nuts.

Spice Cake.
Mrs. Light.

2 cups brown sugar, $\frac{1}{2}$ cup butter, 1 cup thick milk, the yolks of 4 eggs, well beaten; and whites of 2, 1 nutmeg, 1 teaspoon cloves, 1 of cinnamon, 2 cups flour, 1 teaspoon soda.

Delicious Cake.
Mrs. A. M. Ayers.

2 cups pulverized sugar, 1 cup butter, 1 cup corn starch, 2 cups flour, 1 cup sweet milk, 2 teaspoonfuls of Cleveland baking powder, the whites of 6 eggs, flavor with lemon.

Nut Cake.
Mrs. Ira Rutter.

2 cups sugar, 1 cup butter, 1 cup water, 2 cups shellbark kernels, 3 cups flour, 4 eggs, 3 teaspoons Cleveland baking powder.

Cottolene requires only 2-3 the quantity of lard. Use it.

Snowflake Cake.

2 cups sugar, 1 cup of butter, worked to a cream; 1 cup of sweet milk, 1 cup corn starch, 2 teaspoonfuls Cleveland baking powder, mixed in 2 cups of flour; whites of 8 eggs; keep 2 out for icing; flavor with vanilla.

Delicious Cake.
Hannah Phillips, Northumberland.

3 cups of flour, 2 of sugar, ¾ cup sweet milk, whites of 6 eggs, ½ cup butter, teaspoon cream of tartar, ½ teaspoon soda, flavor with lemon.

Snowdrift Cake.
Mrs. M. B. Smith.

2 cups sugar, even full; ½ cup butter, 2½ cups flour, whites of 5 eggs, 1½ teaspoonfuls Cleveland baking powder, 1 cup sweet milk. Beat sugar and butter to a cream, then add the milk, then flour, in which baking powder has been well mixed. Lastly add whites of eggs beaten to a stiff iroth· flavor.

Snowflake Cake.
Mrs. R. S. Spotten.

1 cup of butter, 1 pound pulverized sugar, 1 cup of milk, whites of 4 eggs, 2 cups of flour, and 1 of corn starch; flavor to taste, 3 teaspoons Cleveland baking powder; mix butter and sugar to a cream, then add milk, flour and corn starch, and lastly the whites of eggs. Bake 1 hour in a moderate oven.

Delicious Cake.
Mrs. A. G. Banks, Middletown.

1½ cups granulated sugar, 1 cup butter, 2-3 cup milk, whites of 6 eggs, beaten to a stiff froth; 3 even cups flour, 3 teaspo·nfuls of Cleveland baking powder; flavor with almond; beat well.

Ida Nut Cake.
Mrs. H. Graeff.

2 cups of sugar, 2½ tablespoonfuls of butter, 2 eggs; beat them together; 1 tumblerful of nuts, 2 cups of flour, 2 teaspoonfuls of cream of tartar, mixed with flour; 1 cup of thick milk and 1 teaspoonful of baking soda, stirred in milk; put flour in last.

Cottolene requires only 2-3 the quantity of lard. Use it.

Nut Cake.
F. L. A.

1 cup of butter, 3 cups of white sugar, 5 cups of flour, 1 cup of sweet and sour milk, 4 eggs, 1 pound of currants, 1 cup of broken nuts, 1 lemon, ¼ pound of citron, 1 teaspoon of soda, 2 teaspoons of cream of tartar.

Nut Cake.
Mrs. E. U. Sowers.

1½ cups of sugar, ½ cup of butter, ¾ of a cup of sweet milk, whites of 4 eggs, 2½ cups of flour, 2 teaspoons of Cleveland baking powder, 1 cup of kernels (shellbarks).

Jackson Cake.
Mrs. Ebright.

3 cups sugar, 3 eggs, 1 cup butter, 1 cup sweet milk, 1 teaspoonful soda, 1 of cream of tartar, 4 cups flour.

Eggless Cake.
Mrs. David Harpel.

1 cup butter, 3 cups sugar, 1 pint sour milk or cream, 3 cups flour, 1 pound raisins, teaspoon soda; spice to taste.

Agnes Cake.
Mrs. C. O. Booth.

3 cups sugar, ¾ cup butter, 4 eggs, 1 cup sweet milk, 2 heaping teaspoons Cleveland baking powder, 4 cups of flour.

Cinnamon Cake.
Mrs. Ella D. Moore.

1 cup of sugar, 1 cup of butter, 1 cup of molasses, 1 teaspoonful soda, 4 teaspoonfuls cinnamon, 1 egg, flour to stiffen.

Eight-egg Cake.

1 pound pulverized sugar, ½ pound butter; beat to a cream; beat in eggs, 1 by 1. Almond flavor, ¾ pound flour sifted with a scant ½ teaspoon of Cleveland baking powder.

Spice Cake.
Mrs. Kohr.

2 cups sugar, 1 cup thick milk, 2 cups flour, 1 egg, 1 teaspoonful cinnamon, 1 teaspoonful allspice, 1 teaspoonful ginger, 1 teaspoonful soda.

Cottolene requires only 2-3 the quantity of lard. Use it.

White Lily Cake.
J. R.

Whites of 6 eggs, 2 cups sugar, 3 cups flour, 1 of sweet milk, ½ butter, 2 heaped teaspoons Cleveland baking powder.

Spice Cake.
Mrs. James Watson.

1 cup butter, 2½ cups brown sugar, 2½ cups flour, 2 teaspoonfuls of cinnamon, 2 of allspice, 1½ of ginger, 1½ of cloves, and 1 heaping teaspoonful of soda, a pinch of salt, 1 cup of thick milk, 5 eggs; the whites of the eggs are to beaten separately and added last of all.

Hickorynut Cake.
E. U. Seltzer.

2 cups sugar, ¾ cup butter, 3 eggs, 1 cup thick milk, 1 teaspoon soda, 1 teaspoon cream of tartar, 3 cups flour, 2 cups of nuts.

Spice Cake.
Mrs. Foster.

2 cups brown sugar, 1 cup butter, 1 cup thick milk, 2½ cups flour, 4 eggs, 1½ teaspoons cinnamon, cloves, 1 nutmeg, 1 teaspoon soda.

Chocolate Cake.
Mrs. J. H. Roberts.

2 cups of sugar, 1 cup of butter, whites of 6 eggs, nearly 1 pound flour, 1 cup thick milk, 1 teaspoonful of soda, 2 teaspoonfuls of cream of tartar, Dark part.—1 cup of sugar, ½ cup of butter, yolks of 3 eggs, ½ pound flour; take out ½ cup of flour, add ½ cup of chocolate, ½ cup sweet milk, ½ teaspoonful soda, 1 teaspoonful cream of tartar.

Chocolate Cake.
Mrs. T. S. Walmer.

2 cups sugar, ¾ cup butter, 4 eggs (beaten separately), 1 cup sweet milk, 3 cups flour, 3 teaspoons of Cleveland baking powder; flavor with vanilla.

Icing.—2 ounces chocolate (cut fine and melt), 1 cup white sugar, 2 teaspoons vanilla, 5 tablespoons of milk. Let boil until ropy.

Cottolene requires only 2-3 the quantity of lard. Use it.

Spice Cake.
Mrs. Wm. F. Barton.

¾ cup of butter, 2 cups of sugar, 2 cups of bread sponge, 1 small teaspoonful of soda, 1 teaspoonful of cloves, 1 teaspoonful of cinnamon, 1 teaspoonful of allspice, 2 cups flour, 2 eggs, 1 pound currants. Bake 1 hour and 15 minutes.

Cup Cake.
Mrs. Morris Weidman.

1 generous cup of butter, 2 cups of sugar, 1 small cup of milk, the yolks of 5 eggs, and the whites of 3, 3 cups of flour, 1½ teaspoonfuls of Cleveland baking powder, 1 teaspoonful of flavoring to suit the taste; cream the butter and sugar; then add the milk, next yolks of eggs, next the well beaten whites; lastly the flour, in which the baking powder is sifted.

Cup Cake.
Mrs. Ebright.

1 cup butter, 2 cups of sugar, 3 cups of flour, 2 eggs, 2 teaspoonfuls powder, 1 cup of milk.

Minnehaha Cake.
Julia Lord.

2 cups sugar, ½ cup butter, 1 cup milk, 3 cups flour, 3 teaspoonfuls Cleveland baking powder, whites of 6 eggs; bake in layers. Make boiled icing, add 1 cup of raisins, 1 cup English walnuts and a little vanilla. Spread between with icing on top and sides.

Minnehaha Cake.
Mrs. D. Rodearmel.

3 cups sugar, ¾ cup butter, 5 eggs, 1 cup sweet milk, 3 cups flour, 3 teaspoons Cleveland baking powder.

Feather Cake.

2 cups sugar, 1 cup sweet milk, 2 eggs, 3 cups flour, 2 tablespoons butter, 2 teaspoons Cleveland baking powder.

Pound Cake.
Mrs. W. Richards.

¾ pound butter (1½ cups), 1 pound sugar, 12 eggs, 1 pound flour, 1 teaspoon Cleveland baking powder; use flavor to taste.

Cottolene requires only 2-3 the quantity of lard. Use it.

Soda Pound Cake.
Mrs. S. Reinoehl.

1½ cups sugar, ¾ cups butter, 2 cups flour, ½ cup sweet milk, 4 eggs, 1½ teaspoonfuls Cleveland baking powder; flavor with lemon.

Devil's Food Cake.

2 cups of brown sugar, ½ cup butter, 1-3 cake of chocolate, ½ cup of hot water. Dissolve chocolate in ½ of water, and in the other ½ of water dissolve soda; 1 scant teaspoon of baking soda, 2 cups of flour, 2 eggs, beaten separately.

Icing.—2 cups of brown sugar, ½ cup sweet cream, butter, size of an egg; boil until thick; 1 teaspoon of vanilla; beat until light and clear, then it is ready to spread between cake and ice all around.

Half-pound Cake.
Mrs. Light.

1 pound sugar, ½ butter, 1 pound flour, 6 eggs, 1 cup sweet milk; sugar and butter to a cream, add yolks, well beaten; 2 teaspoons of Cleveland baking powder.

Yankee Pound Cake.

1 cup butter, 3 cups flour, 2 cups sugar, 4 eggs, 1 teaspoonful of soda, 1 cup of sour cream.

Pound Cake.
Mrs. S. Reinoehl.

1 pound sugar, 1 pound butter, mixed to a cream; add the yolks of 10 eggs, well beaten; then add 1 pound flour, 2 teaspoonfuls Cleveland baking powder, whites of the eggs well beaten.

Devil's Food Cake.
Mrs. G. W. Jamieson.

Part 1.—1 cup brown sugar, 2½ cups flour, 3 eggs, yolks; ½ cup butter, ¾ cup sweet milk, 1 teaspoon soda in sifted flour.

Part 2.—1 cup grated chocolate, ½ cup sweet milk, 1 cup brown sugar.

Set part 2 on stove until all is dissolved; do not let boil; when cold stir into part 1. Bake in 2 layers, and put together with chocolate or white frosting; or bake in a loaf.

Cottolene requires only 2-3 the quantity of lard. Use it.

CAKES.

Cold Water Cake.

2 cups sugar, 4 eggs, ¾ cup butter or lard, 1 teaspoon soda, 1 teaspoon cream of tartar, 5 tablespoonfuls of water.

Sugar Cakes.
Mrs. C. M. Light.

1 pound sugar, ½ pound butter, 5 eggs, ½ teacup of thick milk, 1 teaspoon of soda, flour to roll; flavor with lemon drops.

Angel Food.

Whites of 9 large eggs, 1 heaping cup fine granulated sugar, 1 cup flour, sifted 5 times before measuring; ½ teaspoonful cream of tartar, a pinch of salt, ½ teaspoonful each of lemon and vanilla extract; separate eggs, add salt and cream of tartar to the whites and beat till very stiff, add sugar and flavoring, beat thoroughly; then carefully fold in the flour. Put in a moderate oven at once; bake from 40 to 50 minutes in a moderate oven; care should be taken not to stir much when the flour is added, it should be carefully folded in.

Sugar Cakes.
Mrs. F. P. Spiese, Tamaqua.

Line pie tins with pastry, then fill with the following: Mix as you would any other cake, 2 cups sugar, ¼ cup butter, 1 cup cold water, 2¼ cups flour, 2 eggs, 2 teaspoonfuls Cleveland baking powder, sprinkle sugar on top and bake. These are nice for breakfast.

Mrs. Van's Layer Cake.

1¼ cups granulated sugar, 3 eggs, ½ cup butter, ½ cup sweet milk, 2 cups flour, 2 teaspoons Cleveland baking powder. Cream butter and sugar thoroughly; beat yolks to a stiff froth and stir in, then add milk, then beaten whites, then flour; stir hard. This is also desirable baked in 2 square layer pans and iced heavily, to be cut in squares.

Sour Milk Cake.

1 cup raisins, ½ cup of butter, 1 cup of sour milk, 1½ cups of sugar, 3 cups of flour, 1 teaspoonful of soda, 1 egg, spice to suit the taste, nutmeg, cloves, cinnamon.

Cottolene requires only 2-3 the quantity of lard. Use it.

Buckeye Cake.
Mrs. John H. Diehl.

2 cups sugar, 1 cup butter, 4 eggs, 1 teaspoon soda in a little vinegar; flour enough to roll.

Angel Food.
Mrs. S. Reinoehl.

Whites of 9 eggs, well beaten; 1¼ cups sifted granulated sugar, 1 cup sifted flour, ½ teaspoon cream of tartar, a pinch of salt added to eggs before beating; after adding flour stir very lightly; bake in a moderate oven 35 or 50 minutes

Chocolate Layer Cake.
Mrs. Blanche McNeal.

3 eggs, the whites; 2 cups of sugar, 1 cup of sweet milk, 2 large tablespoonfuls of butter, 3 cups of flour, 2 heaping teaspoonfuls Cleveland baking powder. Bake ½ of the batter in 2 pans and to the remaining ½ add ½ cup of grated chocolate. Then bake; when done pile up the layers alternately, light and dark, spreading chocolate icing between.

Chocolate Icing.—Butter, size of an egg, 1 pint brown sugar, ½ cup of milk or water, ½ cake of chocolate. Boil 20 minutes and pour over cake while warm.

Chocolate Cake.
Mrs. Rev. I. C. Fisher.

½ cake of chocolate, mix with ½ cup of milk and yolk of 1 egg, 1 cup of sugar, 1 teaspoonful of vanilla. Boil this a few minutes till sugar and chocolate are well dissolved; let this cool while mixing the cake. 1 cup of sugar, ½ cup of butter, ½ cup of milk, 2 cups of flour, 2 eggs, 1 teaspoonful Cleveland baking powder; add this to the boiled part and bake in tins; put icing between.

Chocolate Cake.
Mrs. Chas. H. Rockel, Allentown.

½ cup butter, ½ cup milk, 1 cup sugar, 2 eggs, or the whites of 4, 1½ cups flour, 1 teaspoon Cleveland baking powder.

Filling.—2 squares Baker's chocolate, ½ cup milk, yolk of 1 egg, sweeten to taste. Boil until thick as jelly; when cold add 1 teaspoon vanilla, and spread cake.

Cottolene requires only 2-3 the quantity of lard. Use it.

Chocolate Cake.
Mrs. W. Klopp.

2 cups of sugar, 1 cup sweet milk, ½ cup of butter, 2 teaspoons Cleveland baking powder, 3 eggs, 3 cups of flour, 3 tablespoonfuls of chocolate.

Chocolate Marble Cake.
Miss Kreider.

3 cups sugar, 1 cup butter, 4 cups flour, 1 cup milk, 3 teaspoons Cleveland baking powder, 4 eggs; grate chocolate in ½ the dough.

Icing.—1 pound pulverized sugar, 3 eggs, ½ cake melted chocolate.

Chocolaate Cake
Esther J. Boyer.

1 cup butter, 3 cups sugar, 7 eggs, ¾ cup thick milk 1 teaspoon baking soda, 3½ cups flour, 1 teaspoon cream of tartar. Take sugar, butter and yolks of eggs, cream well; then add the rest, keeping the whites of 3 eggs for icing. Take 1-3 of the dough; grate in chocolate; bake in quick oven.

GINGER BREADS.

Mother's Gingerbread.
Mrs. G. W. Jamieson.

1 egg, 1 cup molasses, 1 cup sugar, (brown or white), 1 scant cup of lard or butter, 1 cup of sour milk or butter-milk, 2 teaspoonfuls soda in a little hot water; salt and spice to taste; ginger and cinnamon. Make thick batter with flour.

Molasses Gingerbread.

1 cup New Orleans molasses, 1 cup sugar, ½ cup shortening, 1 cup water, 1 large teaspoon soda, dissolved in the water; 1 teaspoon ginger, ½ teaspoon cinnamon, 1 quart flour. Stir molasses, sugar, shortening and spices together thoroughly, then add water and flour. If too thin, stir in a little flour.

Cottolene requires only 2-3 the quantity of lard. Use it.

Soft Gingerbread.
Mrs. John T. Atkins.

1 cup of sugar, 1 cup of thick milk, 3 cups of flour, ½ cup of New Orleans molasses, ½ cup of lard and butter, 2 eggs, 1 teaspoon of cinnamon, 1 teaspoon of cloves, 1 teaspoon of ginger, 1 teaspoon of nutmeg, 1 teaspoon of cream of tartar, 2 teaspoons of soda.

Soft Gingerbread.

1 cup of butter, 1 cup of sugar, 1 cup of molasses, 1 cup of milk, 3 eggs, 4 cups of flour, 1 teaspoonful soda, 1 teaspoonful cream of tartar. Mix all together and bake in a moderate oven.

Gingerbread.
Mrs. D. S. Herr, Pleasant Grove.

3 eggs, 1 tincup of molasses, ½ tincup butter or lard, ½ tincup sweet cream, small tablespoon soda, dissolved in a little vinegar; 1 teaspoon cream of tartar, 4 teacups flour, 1 tablespoon ginger.

Gingerbread.
Mrs. S.

1 cup molasses, 1 cup sugar, 1 cup butter and lard, 1 cup thick milk, 3 eggs, 1 teaspoon soda, 1 teaspoon each of cinnamon, ginger and cloves. Bake ½ hour in a moderate oven.

Soft Gingerbread.
Manda Hottenstein.

1 pint molasses, 1 cup of brown sugar, ¾ cup melted lard, 1 cup sour milk, 2 eggs, 1 tablespoon of soda; flour to stiffen. Pour on flat tins.

Soft Gingerbread.
Mrs. Hopewell.

Small ½ cup butter, 1½ cups molasses, 2 well beaten eggs, 3 cups flour, 1 tablespoonful ginger, a little each of nutmeg, allspice and cinnamon; ½ cup sour milk, 1 teaspoon soda.

Gingerbread.
Mrs. A. G. Banks, Middletown.

1 cup molasses, 1 cup sour milk, ½ cup sugar (brown), 1 egg, butter, size of an egg; 1 even teaspoonful of soda, ginger to suit the taste. Flour to make a batter. Bake in loaf or in gem tins.

Cottolene requires only 2-3 the quantity of lard. Use it.

CANDY.

Good Chocolate Candy.

½ pound brown sugar, ½ cup dark molasses, 2 ounces butter, ¼ cake Baker's chocolate, ½ cup milk; boil slowly; tablespoon vinegar.

Butter Scotch.
Mrs. A. D. Smith.

2 cups light brown sugar, ¾ cup best table molasses, (not New Orleans) 1-3 cup of hot water. Boil together hard for 15 minutes. Then add a pinch of soda and ½ pound of best table butter, and boil until it crisps when dropped in cold water; add 2 teaspoons vanilla and 2 cups of chopped shell barks, and pour in tins, which must not be buttered.

Chocolate Caramels.
Mrs. J. K. Fisher.

1 cake of Baker's chocolate, ½ pound butter, 2½ pounds of granulated sugar, 2 teacups milk; put all in skillet together and stir constantly, after it comes to a boil. Boil steadily but not too hard for about 20 minutes; just before removing from the stove add vanilla to taste. Have buttered pans ready; score in blocks, with the back of a knife.

Chocolate Caramels.
Esther J. Boyer.

1 pound sugar, ¼ pound butter, ½ cup sweet milk, 3 ounces of chocolate. Put sugar, milk and chocolate into a pan, let it come to a boil, then add butter; flavor with vanilla. Pour into pans, greased with butter, then beat until thick and smooth. Cut into small squares.

Cream Chocolates.
Mrs. E. U. Sowers.

2 cups of sugar, 1 cup of water, 1½ tablespoons of corn starch; boil 12 minutes; beat until sugary, arrange in drops and roll in melted chocolate. Do not stir the syrup.

Hickorynut Kisses.

1 pound sugar, 1 pound nuts, 1 tablespoon of flour, whites of 6 eggs. Roll the nuts very fine; beat the whites, add the sugar; beat well, add the nuts, then the flour.

Cream Walnuts.
Mrs. J. K. Fisher.

Mix 1 pound of XXXX sugar with the beaten white of 1 egg, and 1 tablespoon of water; take kernels of English walnuts, press 1 on each side of the block. Dates or figs may be used in the same way.

Chocolate Caramels.
Mrs. E. U. Sowers.

¾ of a pound of sugar (white), ¼ of a pound of butter, 1 cup of sweet milk, 6 tablespoons of molasses, 6 tablespoons of chocolate.

Peanut Taffy.
Lottie T. Barton, Tamaqua.

1 cup of molasses (syrup), 1 cup white sugar, ¼ cup vinegar; when done add a piece of butter, size of a walnut, and ½ teaspoonful of baking soda, and 1 pint of peanuts; vanilla flavoring.

Cocoanut Drops.
C. W. Cyphers, Minneapolis, Minn.

1 pound cocoanut, ½ pound powdered sugar and the white of 1 egg. Work all together and roll into little balls in the hand; bake on buttered tins.

Chocolate Caramels.
Mrs. F.

1 cup milk, 2 pounds sugar, 1 small cocoanut (grated fine); boil milk, sugar and cocoanut together until stiff, pour into shallow pans, cut in squares. When taken from the fire, before putting in the pans, add a teaspoonful of vanilla.

Troche for the Throat.

1 pound of pulverized sugar, 4 ounces pulverized licorice, 1 ounce pulverized cubeb, 2 ounces pulverized gum arabic; wet with a little water, flavor with Wintergreen Oil; roll in corn starch, cut thin with a thimble; put away to dry.

CANDY.

Cocoanut Candy.
E. U. Seltzer.

1 pound of brown sugar, 6 tablespoonfuls of water, 6 tablespoonfuls New Orleans molasses; boil a little while before putting in the cocoanut.

Butter Scotch.
Mrs. F.

2 large cups brown sugar, ½ cup water, ½ cup butter. Cook until it snaps.

Chocolate Caramels.
Mrs. Wm. Loser.

1½ cups chocolate, ¾ cup molasses, ½ pound butter, 1 cup sweet cream, 1 pound sugar.

Chocolate Caramels.

¼ cake of chocolate, ½ pint of milk or cream, 1 cup of sugar, ½ cup of butter, ½ cup of molasses; flavor with vanilla and boil 28 minutes.

Chocolate Caramels.

1 pound sugar, white; 1 cup milk, tablespoon butter, ½ cake of Baker's chocolate; boil till thick. Pour in shallow pans; cut in square blocks.

Mrs. Joslyn's Candy.
Mrs. J. C. Urich, Marquette, Mich.

2 cups brown sugar, 2 cups granulated sugar, 2 cups N. O. molasses, teaspoon butter, ½ cup cocoanut. Boil until it threads; pour into buttered pans about ½ inch thick; when cold cut in squares.

Cream Chocolates.
Mrs. Paine.

1¼ pounds XXXX sugar, white of 1 egg, 1 spoonful water; mix like pie dough, put on buttered tins for a day; then melt some chocolate in a cup, add a little butter and sugar to melt it, then dip the cream in.

Home-made Candy.
Mrs. H. T. Atkins.

1 pound soft white sugar, butter, the size of a walnut; ½ glass of water; flavor with vanilla. Boil until brittle; do not stir. Pour in buttered pans until cool enough to draw.

CANDY.

Peppermint Candy.
Martha Karch.

1 pound of confectionary sugar, the white of 1 egg, 2 tablespoons of water; mix all well together; peppermint to flavor: do not boil.

Cocoanut Candy.
Mrs. J. K. Fisher.

2 pounds of soft white sugar, 1 small cocoanut, grated; 1 cup of sweet milk, butter, size of a walnut; boil till stiff.

Cocoanut Caramels.
Mrs. J. K. Fisher.

2 pounds of sugar, ½ cake chocolate, ½ cup of molasses, ½ cup sweet milk, butter, size of a walnut; 1 tablespoon of flour; when done flavor with vanilla.

Peanut Kisses.
E. D. M.

1 egg, 1 cup soft sugar, 2 tablespoons of milk, 1 cup peanuts chopped fine; flour to make as stiff as nut cake.

M. L. LOWRY,

Manufacturer of **Pretzels,** Plain and ...Fancy **Cakes**

Bread and Pastry...

ALSO DEALER IN

Confectioneries

and **Ice Cream . . .**

All Orders Promptly Filled

743 Cumberland Street, Lebanon, Pa.

MISCELLANEOUS RECEIPTS.

Best Cough Syrup.
Louisa C. Light.

Take 5 cents licorice, 5 cents rock candy, 5 cents gum arabic, 1 pint of water; boil them to ¾ of a pint; when cold take 5 cents of paragoric and 5 cents of Antemonial wine; bottle it. Take 1 teaspoonful 4 times a day.

To Clean Paint.
Sarah T. Paul.

Put a ½ peck of bran into a washboiler, and fill it with cold water, set it over the fire and boil for ½ hour; then strain through a sieve a bucket 1-3 full; put as much cold water to it as you have of the bran-water, and use with a soft scrubbing-brush or if the paint is not very much soiled, a soft flannel cloth, but no soap. It will make the paint look like new. Keep the remainder on the stove boiling hot to renew with.

Toothache Liniment.
Louisa C. Light.

A sure cure for sick headache, neuralgia and rheumatism, Take ½ pint alcohol, 1 ounce gumcamphor, 1 ounce choloform, 1 ounce hartshorn; put the camphor in the alcohol and after it is all dissolved, add the chloroform and hartshorn. Use this freely on the face and teeth.

Toothache Liniment.
Louisa C. Light.

Take 1 pint of spirits of turpentine; add ½ ounce of camphor. Let it stand till the camphor is dissolved, then rub on the part affected and it will never fail. Flannels should be applied; repeat it morning and evening.

To Cleanse the Hair.
H. M. M.

Beat up the yolk of an egg with a pint of soft water; apply it warm; rub well, and afterward rinse with clean, soft water.

MISCELANEOUS RECEIPTS.

To Expel Ants.
Mrs. Julia Wright.

Ants of all kinds, also roaches, can be expelled by using powdered borax. If soot gets on the carpet sprinkle salt on it, and with a dust pan and brush you can remove all the soot; repeat if necessary.

House Insects.
Mrs. Julia Wright.

No insect which usually infests the house and crawls over the floors or woodwork can live under the application of hot alum water. It will destroy red and black ants, cockroaches, spiders, and chinchbugs. Take 2 pounds of alum and dissolve in 3 or 4 quarts of boiling water. Let it stand on the fire to melt, then apply it with a brush, while nearly boiling hot, to every joint and crevice in your closet, bedstead, pantry shelves, etc. If, in whitewashing, plenty of alum is added, it will keep off insects.

To Cure Meat.

For 25 pounds of meat, 1 quart of fine salt, 1 tablespoon of salt petre, enough molasses to make the color of light brown sugar. Mix together and rub on the meat. Pack it tight, let it stand 48 hours and hang up.

For Hoarseness.
Louisa C. Light.

4 ounces of grated horseradish, 1 pint of good cider vinegar; let stand over night, then add ½ pint of honey and bring to a boiling point, then strain and squeeze out. Dose, 1 to 2 teaspoons several times a day; very good for hoarseness, loss of voice and all colds.

Frost Bites.
Mrs. Julia Wright.

The following is a simple remedy for frost bites: Extract the frost by the application of ice water till the frozen part is pliable, but let no artificial heat touch it; then apply a salve made of equal parts of hog's lard and gunpowder, rubbed together until it forms a paste, and in less than 4 hours the frozen parts will be well.

For a Cough
H. M. M.

Roast a lemon very carefully, without burning it. When it is thoroughly hot, cut and squeeze the juice into a cup over 2 tablespoonfuls of powdered sugar. Dose, a tablespoonful.

Simple Remedy for Rheumatism.
H. M. M.

Bathe the parts affected with water (in which potatoes have been boiled), as hot as can be borne. This has been tested, and found to be very efficacious.

Cure for Lock Jaw.
R. Moore.

Take a small quantity of turpentine, warm it, and pour it on the wound (no matter where the wound is or what its nature is) and relief will follow in a few minutes. Turpentine is also a sovereign remedy for croup. Saturate a piece of flannel with it, and place the flannel on the throat or chest—and in very severe cases, 3 to 5 drops on a lump of sugar may be taken internally.

Cure for Erysipelas.
Anna M. Hammer.

Dilute the mother tincture of belladonna, 1 teaspoonful to $\frac{1}{2}$ a glass of warm water. Wet an old linen handkerchief and apply to the parts, renewing whenever dry. Take pellets of belladonna internally, prepared homeopathically.

How to Preserve Eggs.
Mrs. J. K. Fisher.

To each pailful of water, add 2 pints of fresh slacked lime, and 1 pint of common salt; mix well. Fill your barrel $\frac{1}{2}$ full with this fluid, place the eggs in it any time after June and they will keep for 2 years if desired.

Furniture Varnish.
Mrs. D. M. Karmany.

2 parts of linseed oil to 1 of kerosene; rub on with a flannel rag thoroughly. Let stand awhile, then with a clean piece of flannel polish until it shines. This does not injure the daintiest wood. Odor soon evaporates.

How to Remedy a Few Annoyances.
H. M. Miller.

To drive red ants out of a cupboard, place in it an earthen dish containing a pint of tar, over which 2 quarts of hot water have been poured.

If irons be rough and sticky, rub them on fine salt sprinkled on a board.

A spoonful of vinegar put into the water in which meats or fowls are boiled makes them tender.

Simple Remedy for Croup.
Mrs. M. E. Banks, Chambersburg.

A teaspoonful of glycerine and water mixed will loosen the cough in a few minutes; if not, give a second dose.

To Keep Butter Fresh.
Mrs. Mary Weaver.

Work until solid, make into rolls; take 2 gallons of water, 1 pint white sugar, 1 level tablespoonful saltpetre; make the brine strong enough with salt to bear an egg. Boil and skim. Let cool, pour over butter and keep under brine with a weight. Butter will thus keep for a year as sweet as when churned.

Care of Oil Paintings and Frames.
Mrs. E. B. Price.

Wash the picture when necessary in sweet milk and warm water, drying carefully. Give the gilt frame when new a coat of white varnish and all specks can then be washed off with water or suds without harm.

To Remove Sunburn.
Mrs. Mary R. Collins.

Scrape a cake of brown Windsor soap to a powder, add 1 ounce each of eau de Cologne and lemon juice; mix well and form into cakes. This removes tan, prevents hand from chapping and makes the skin soft and white.

Fly Paper.
R. Moore.

Coat paper with turpentine varnish, and oil it to keep the varnish from drying.

MISCELANEOUS RECEIPTS.

Household Hints.
H. M. M.

Orange peel dried and grated makes excellent flavoring for cakes and puddings.

A cup of cold boiled rice added to any griddle cakes or muffins makes them lighter and more wholesome.

Wash for Sunburn.

Carbolic acid, camphor, glycerine, rose water.

Cure for Neuralgia.

½ drachm sal-ammonia in 1 ounce of camphor water. Take a teaspoonful several times 5 minutes apart until relieved. Another simple remedy is horseradish; grate and mix in vinegar the same as for table purposes, and apply to the temple when the face or head is affected, or to the wrist when the pain is in the arm or shoulder.

Chicken Powder.

2 ounces of saltpetre, ½ pound flower of sulphur, ½ cayenne pepper. Dose, 1 to 2 tablespoons once a week for 10 or 15 chickens. Very good for chickens.

Inflamed Eyes.
Anna M. Hammer.

Make and boil starch just as for laundry purposes. Have thick enough to spread on a cloth. Bind this on the eyes as hot as one can bear, and renew when cold and stiff.

To Wash White Flannels.
Mrs. M. E. Banks, Chambersburg.

Wash in cold water. Make a good suds with any washing soap; put in ½ teaspoonful of powdered borax to a bucketful of water to wash the garment. Don't rub soap on garment; add more soap to water if required; let soak ½ hour, rinse and hang up.

Wash for the Hands.
H. M. M.

1 ounce refined borax, 1 ounce of cologne, 1 tablespoonful glycerine, 1 wine glass of water, 2 tablespoonfuls lemon juice. Put all together in a bottle and shake well,

Remedy for Croup.
Mrs. M. E. Banks, Chambersburg.

A teaspoonful of syrup or common molasses and castor oil given when the first hoarse cough is heard . Usually the first dose will loosen the cough and the little one will sleep. If not, follow with a second dose.

Burns.

For a burn nothing is better than baking soda, spread on thick and dry. Cover lightly to keep out the air.

Indigo.
Mrs. Julia Wright.

A good recipe for indigo. 2 ounces oxalic acid, 1 ounce Prussian blue, pulverized; add 1 quart of soft water; mix well and bottle for use.

To Pack Eggs for Winter.
Anna Hottenstein.

1 quart of air slacked lime, 4 quarts boiling water, 1 tablespoon of cream of tartar. Cool and drop eggs in.

Tar Cordial.

2 pounds granulated sugar, 1½ pounds rock candy, 1 pint cider vinegar, ½ pint tar. Simmer for 3 days. Take a stick and remove the thick skin of tar on the top; strain and bottle.

Soda Mint.
Mrs. S. Y. Karmany.

1 pint of water, 1 tablespoonful aromatic spirits of ammonia, 1 tablespoon of soda, 1 tablespoon of essence of peppermint. Take a teaspoonful after meals for indigestion.

In Using Cloves.

In using cloves for pickles or preserves the blossom end should always be removed, as this always darkens the liquid in using.

THE SICK ROOM.

Perfect Love.
R. Moore.

1 tablespoonful of sugar, 1 slice each of orange and lemon; fill the tumbler 1-3 full of shaved ice and fill balance with water. Vanilla syrup adds very much to its taste.

Arrowroot Custard.

1 tablespoon of arrowroot, 1 pint of milk, 1 egg, 2 tablespoons sugar; mix the arrowroot with a little of the cold milk; put the rest of the milk on the fire and boil and stir in the arrowroot and egg and sugar, well beaten together; scald and pour into cups to cool; any flavor the invalid prefers may be added.

Junket.

3 quarts of milk, luke-warm, sweeten to taste and flavor. Stir it up well; have ready a piece of rennet; wash it and lay it in a bowl with a small teacup of warm water. Let it soak for 15 or 20 minutes. Then pour the water into milk, let it stand to stiffen; when stiff grate nutmeg over it.

Chicken Panada.

Skin the chicken and cut it up in joints. Take all the meat off the bones and cut up into small pieces; put it in a jar with a little salt, tie it down, and set it in a saucepan of boiling water. It should boil from 4 to 6 hours; then pass it through a sieve with a little of the broth. It could be made in a hurry in 2 hours, but is better when longer time is allowed. Do not put the wings in the panada.

Soup for Invalids.

Cut in small pieces 1 pound of mutton; boil it gently in 2 quarts of water; take off the scum, and when reduced to a pint, strain it. Season with salt and take a cupful at a time.

Tamarind Whey.
Mrs. R. S. Malsberger.

A cooling and somewhat laxative drink is made by putting 2 tablespoonfuls of the fruit into a pint of milk, while it is boiling, stirring the mixture well, and then straining it. It should not be used until cool and should always be freshly made.

Common Sweet Juice.

Into a pint of water stir a paste made of a tablespoonful of corn starch or flour, rubbed smooth with a little cold water, ad i a cupful of sugar and a tablespoonful of vinegar; cook well for 3 minutes; take from the fire and add a piece of butter as large as an egg; when cool flavor with a tablespoonful of vanilla or lemon extract.

Drinks for Invalids.

Mash any kind of fruit, currants, tamarinds, berries, pour boiling water on them; in 10 minutes strain it off, sweeten and let cool; add a little ice; do not allow the drink to stand in the sick-room; keep it in a cool, airy place.

Cream of Tartar Drink.

2 spoonfuls cream of tartar, 1 grated rind of lemon, ½ cup of white sugar, and 1 pint of boiling water, is a good summer drink for invalids, and is cleansing to the blood.

Wheat Fruinty.

Boil wheat to a jelly; to 1 quart of jelly add 1 quart milk, 3 eggs; sweeten and flavor to taste; scald together and use hot or cold milk.

Raspberry Vinegar.

1 quart of raspberries, cover them with good vinegar; the next morning add another quart of berries, press them down with a spoon; continue so every morning until you have enough, then strain; add 1 pound of sugar to 1 pint of juice, put on stove, just let it come to a boil. Bottle and cork when cool.

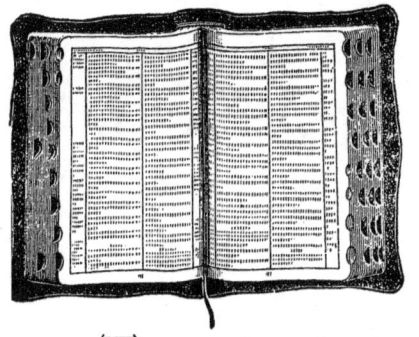

W̲HEN e'er you take this little book
And on its dainty pages look,
Upon this page please cast your eye,
Nor pass my advertisement by....

J. A. DEHUFF,
Bookseller and Stationer,
LEBANON, PA.

T̲'IS here all sorts of books you'll find
To suit all ages of mankind,
The preacher, the lawyer, the sad undertaker,
The butcher,
The baker,
The candlestick maker.

N̲O NEED to go down to John Moneymaker,
Books that teach you to fast,—how to make a good dinner,
Books that will suit both the saint and the sinner,
Books old and rare and wondrous cheap,
Enough to make a willow weep.

C̲ALL there and you'll see at a glance,
"A Lady of Quality" with a "Gentleman of France,"
"A Prisoner of Zehnda" and "John Applegate, Freeman,"
And "Three Muskateers" with "Three Jolly Seamen,"
While "The Man in Black" in his garments of night,
Stands boldly aside " The Woman in White."
To "Lots" of others, they will call your attention,
But (like articles of a public sale)
They're too numerous to mention.

T̲HEN his wall paper, too, its the wonder for miles,
So good, and so cheap, and the *sweetest* of styles.

S̲EE his window shades! Here you *will* stop,
You are dumb with amazement!
Quiet? Well I should smile!
Why there for a while
It's so quiet you can almost hear a "dew drop."
We have blinds that are plain, blinds with fringe, blinds with lace,
We have blinds which I'm sure all your windows would grace,
And would make men, women and children all stare,
And declare,
That where'er
They had been that they ne'er
Had seen aught in their lives that at all would compare,
With such elegant shades, why that they would "swear."
You'd be the envy of people who purchase elsewhere.

A̲ND now I have said, I think, just enough.
Remember the store of **J. A. DeHuff,**
Make your purchases there, and from night and morn,
(And *vice versa*) you'll thank your stars that you ever were born.

INDEX.

	PAGE
Biscuits, Buns, etc.,	99
Bread,	91
Cakes,	131
" Small,	105
Candy,	173
Desserts,	69
Entrees,	37
Ginger Breads,	171
Ices and Creams,	79
Icings,	95
Jams, Jellies, etc.,	97
Meats,	25
Miscellaneous Receipts,	177
Oysters and Fish,	22
Omelets and Toasts,	47
Pickles,	115
Pies,	85
Preserves, Jellies, etc.,	127
Puddings,	49
Salads,	41
Small Cakes,	105
Soups,	17
The Sick Room,	183
Table of Measures,	14
Vegetables,	31

Winter

The Wintry Season brings many troubles to persons with weak throats and to those who use their voices much in public speaking or singing. All affected with throat troubles find nothing better than

Boger's Throat and Voice Troches.

Rev. Warren J. Johnson, one of Lebanon's most eloquent divines, has this to say of them:

THEIR EFFECT IS ALMOST INSTANTANEOUS.

Having used various troches for my throat. I cheerfully bear unprejudiced testimony to the excellence and efficiency of Boger's. I have found them most effective in relieving hoarseness, clearing the throat and strengthening the vocal chords. Their effect is almost instantaneous and the taste pleasing.

REV. WARREN J. JOHNSON,
Lebanon, Pa., Sept. 15, '94.   Pastor St. John's Church.

All the Year Round

Most of us prefer good cakes, etc., but no matter how good the cook is, her work will not be pleasing to the ones whom she works for unless she uses pure Baking Soda, Cream of Tartar, Spices and Flavors. We keep only that kind, and at fair prices.

Summer

Melons, Fruit and Bad Water cause Bowel Troubles at this season, but if you use

Boger's Diarrhoea and Cholera Mixture

you have no cause to fear serious results.

Read what **Mr. Mann** tells of its virtues:

Have been for many years a sufferer from Chronic Diarrhoea. I have tried all sorts of remedies, but they did no good. I thank God that I am at last cured; positively cured. I used Boger's Diarrhoea and Cholera Mixture. It is with great pleasure that I recommend it to ones afflicted as I was.

JOSEPH MANN, Eighth and Locust Sts.

...25c. a Bottle...

Boger's Drug Store, 47 S. EIGHTH ST,.
LEBANON, PA.

Cut Prices on Patent Medicines

HIGH GRADE...

Carriage Goods and Horse Clothing

Buggies
Carriages
Phaetons

Bicycles, Guns, Revolvers, Etc.
BICYCLE SUITS, SWEATERS, STOCKINGS, BELTS, ETC.

E. M.
Hottenstein,
Cor. Ninth
and Willow Streets,
LEBANON, PA.

Fine Hand=Made
Easy Fitting Shoes

DAVID F. WISE,
...720 Cumberland Street.

→ MAKER OF ←

Fine Custom Boots and Shoes

All the Finest Grades, and Satisfaction Guaranteed.

Particular attention given to odd-shaped feet.
Easy-Fitting Shoes for corns and bunions.
Headquarters for all kinds of Shoe Dressings and Blacking.
Also manufacturer of Boot, Shoe and Gaiter Uppers and dealer in **Leather and Shoe Findings.**

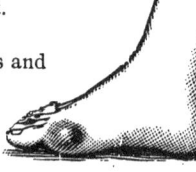

S. G. Valentine.

 Groceries.

IF YOU WANT INGREDIENTS FOR YOUR RECIPES THAT ARE PURE AND WHOLESOME, WE ARE PREPARED TO MEET YOUR NEEDS. . . . .
☛ WE CALL YOUR SPECIAL ATTENTION TO OUR

Olive Oil.

DIRECTLY IMPORTED BY US, AND OF THE VERY FINEST GRADE. . . . .

"If it's anything nice, we have it."

838 Cumberland St., Lebanon, Pa.

These Days —

everybody wants to buy the best for the least money. If in want of . . . .

Clothing

we invite you to our store and inspect our stock. We keep nothing but the best made and up-to-date kind, and sell them at the lowest prices that similar goods can be sold. A visit to our store will convince you of all we claim,

viz: Lowest Prices and ....Best Made Goods.

C. K. LIGHT, Central One-Price Clothing House,

Opp. Court House, 806 Cumberland St., Lebanon, Pa.

...THE OLDEST BANK IN LEBANON VALLEY...

IN ACTIVE OPERATION SINCE 1831.

Lebanon National Bank

DEPOSITS, $650,000
LOANS, - $750,000

Cor. 9th and Cumberland Sts.
—LEBANON, PA.

Capital, Surplus and Profits,
$360,000.⁰⁰

...SAFE DEPOSIT BOXES TO RENT...

President, THOS. L. BECKER   Cashier, JAMES M. GOSSLER

...Our Prices are the Lowest

We keep...
A full line of desirable

...Footwear

For Men
Women
and Children

Embracing
The Latest Designs in
Up=to=Date Shoemaking

...A call from you and your friends will be appreciated. ....

C. W. Few,

A Department in
C. Shenk's Dry Goods Store.

...Opposite Court House.

Mount Gretna...

On the Line of the
Cornwall & Lebanon Railroad

The Finest Mountain Resort ...and Summer Excursion Grounds In the State.

THE location of the Pennsylvania Chautauqua, Campmeeting of the United Brethren, and Mt. Gretna Agricultural, Mechanical and Industrial Exposition.

 The Park with all its beauties and unrivalled conveniences and facilities free for Excursions.

 **The Cornwall & Lebanon Railroad,** in connection with the Pennsylvania Railroad, form the best Passenger and Freight Route to all points.

For further particulars, address

A. D. Smith,

Lebanon, Pa.   General Superintendent.

In Season and In the Lead

WHAT is of the greatest moment just now to the ladies is, Where can the largest variety of Seasonable Goods be had? Where can we get the most for our money? is a query which, this season above all others, demands a goodly share of consideration.

Every Department in our store is complete, well stocked and well attended. People say this is an "off year." Not so in Dry Goods. We show a stock this season which proves that never in the history of merchandising has such advancement been shown by manufacturers. The words Perfection and Novelty speak volumes.

In Coats and Wraps, in Dress Goods, in every Department, we can conscientiously say that the "times" have stimulated us to an increased activity. Our display of goods has never equalled the present. To discriminating readers our announcements must tally well with evident truths.

...C. Shenk...

816=822 Cumberland Street,

LEBANON, PA.

The North-Western Mutual Life Insurance Company,
MILWAUKEE, WIS.

Organized 1857.

A Purely Mutual Company.

Cash Assets,	Liabilities,	Surplus,
$82,902,389.64.	$66,388,828.38	$16,513,561.26.

Issues All Kinds of Popular and Approved Policies, including Installments, Annuities, Etc.

Dividends to Policy=Holders

....Unequaled.

For further information and testimony of policy-holders as to merits of Company, apply to

H. T. ATKINS, Manager,   LEBANON, PA.

A. C. ZIMMERMAN,

Dealer in

Carpets,

Rugs and Oil=Cloths.

No. 758 Cumberland Street,
LEBANON, PENNA.

John W. Roberts,

DEALER IN

Wall... Paper

Window Shades and Room Mouldings.

No. 127 North Ninth Street,
LEBANON, PA.

By Chance

we might serve any woman once, but when we serve the same woman repeatedly—that is to say—regularly—it stands to reason that our Groceries please them. We would like to add your name to the list of people that we make a particular effort to please. May we hope to do so?

D. B. BUCK,

10th and Church Sts.

Evening Report
...The Ideal Home Paper...

DELIVERED by Carriers every evening except .. Sunday at 6 cents a .. week.............

First in News. . . . .
First in Enterprise. . . . . .
First in the hearts of the People.

Published every Wednesday and Saturday at $1 a year in advance.

Semi=Weekly Report
...The People's Paper...

All the News from County and State, and Departments for each member of the Family. . . . .

Book and Job
Neat
Cheap
Prompt

Printing

The Best Equipped Job Printing Office in the East, outside of .. Philadelphia. . . . .

Anything in the Printing Line, from the smallest card to the largest book.

Paper of Every Description, by the sheet, pound, or ton.

Blank Books
and Stationery
Wholesale and Retail

Writing Paper and Envelopes, 6 cents per box. . . . . . .
Envelopes, 3 cents per pack.
Writing Tablets, 1c. to 30c. .

Report Publishing Company
Report Building, 41 N. Ninth Street LIMITED

LEBANON, PA.

New Commonwealth Shoe Store...

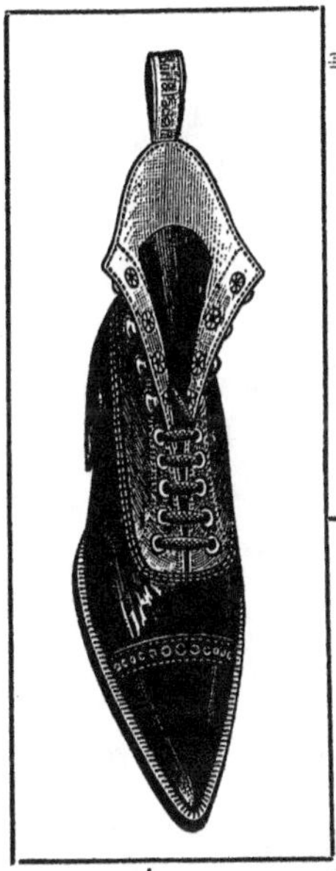

753 Cumberland Street, Lebanon, Pa.

Sons of America Building.

Leading Shoe House.

•••

Largest Stock.

•••

Lowest Prices.

Wholesale and Retail.

Hean & Molly, Proprietors.

The Leading Photographers...

Rise & Gates,

142 North Eighth Street,

Picture Frames...
  A Specialty.

Lebanon, Pa.

You Will Always Find
Fashionable
Millinery

Also a Full Line of
 Butterick Patterns.

AT **Seabold's,**

746 Cumberland Street.

We Guarantee Satisfaction.
        Correct Styles and Low Prices.

Harry G. Arentz,
...The Family Grocer

A Full Line of BAKING POWDERS and SPICES, BOTTLED AND CANNED GOODS, and Everything that is Good to Eat. . . . .

Cor. 4th and Chestnut Sts.,

LEBANON, PA.

W. H. B. MOORE,

Wholesale and Retail Manufacturing Confectioner

...ALSO DEALER IN ALL KINDS OF...

Fruits, Nuts, Etc....

AND A FULL LINE OF

Dolls and Tree Ornaments

Weddings and Parties Supplied with Ice Cream at Short Notice.

Cor. Seventh and Lehman Sts.

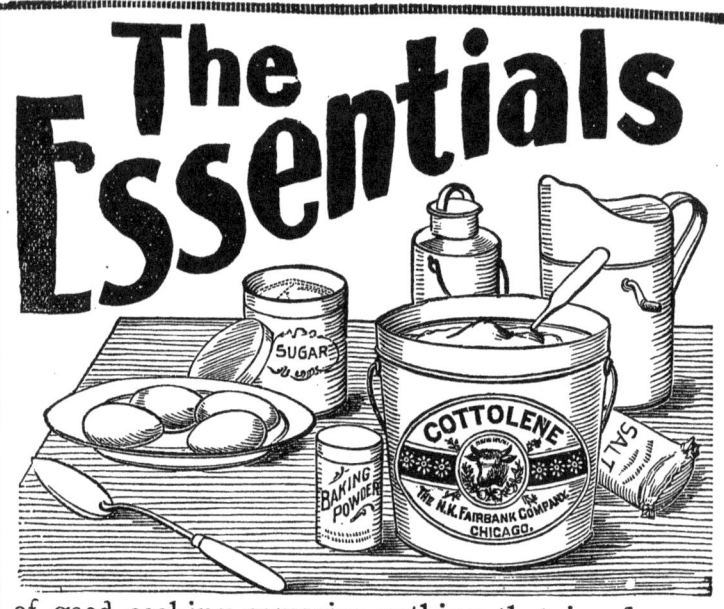

of good cooking comprise nothing that is of more importance than good shortening. Your food will be deliciously light and free from the greasiness and richness that make lard so objectionable if shortened with or fried in pure, clean, sweet

Cottolene

Look for the Cottolene trade marks—"*Cottolene*" and *steer's head in cotton-plant wreath*—on every tin.

THE N. K. FAIRBANK COMPANY,

Chicago, St. Louis, New York, Boston, Philadelphia, San Francisco, New Orleans. Montreal.

Fruit Mixture
Mixture of grape fruit, bits banana & orange.

Salade
Two heads Celery, three hard boiled eggs, mixed with mayonnaise.

Salade
Cooked chicken, 1 head celery, 2 hard boiled eggs mixed with mayonnaise

Fruit Cock-tail.
bits of orange, bananas & fine ap flavored with brandy

Frozen Strawberries
2 boxes Strawberries, crushed and put through a sieve, sweeten & mix with whites of white of five eggs, a tea spoonful lemon juice.

Salade
3 large tomatoes pealed & sliced, large slice on plate and spread with may, then on this large slice of American cheese. Then second slice then lettuce & some may. on top.

Fruit Salade

www.ingramcontent.com/pod-product-compliance
Lightning Source LLC
Chambersburg PA
CBHW051741230426
43670CB00012B/2109